CHASING 100

HOW TO SURPASS YOUR LIMITS AND MASTER THE ART OF REACHING FULL POTENTIAL

Volume 1

Presented by

Andy Henriquez

In Collaboration with Other
Leading Voices as Co-Authors

CROSSBEAM
BOOKS & PUBLISHING

Copyright © 2025 Show Up for Your Life, LLC
Library of Congress Control Number: 2024923815
Published in the United States by Crossbeam Books, LLC, Florida

All rights reserved. Printed in the United States of America.
No part of this book may be used or reproduced in any manner whatsoever without written permission from the author.

All contributors to this work have duly consented to the use of their personal data, facts, recollections, memories, and/or experiences found herein. They are aware that the end and intended result was mass production and publication in connection with this work. As such, they have agreed without equivocation or caveat to indemnify, defend, and hold harmless the collaborator and publisher of this material, along with their affiliates, officers, directors, employees, and agents from any and all claims, damages, expenses, and liabilities arising out of or in connection with the use of such personal data, facts, recollections, memories, and experiences, including any claims of infringement of intellectual property rights or violation of privacy rights.

ISBN: 9798304176842

CONTENTS

CHASING 100: EXPECT TO BE TESTED
By Andy Henriquez 1

YOU DON'T GET TO DEFINE ME
By Althea Payne-Butler 9

I HAD A DADDY ALL ALONG
By Angeleen Harris 15

ALL STEPS ARE MIGHTY!
By Brian H. Nicholas, LAc 21

WHEN ENOUGH BECAME EVERYTHING
By Charese L. Josie 27

EMBRACING MY TRUE REFLECTION
By Darlene L. Thorne, MDiv 33

WEARING A MASK OF STRENGTH
By Dashana Jefferies 41

YOU ARE NOT THEM
By Elaine Robinson Beattie 49

DREAMS DO COME TRUE
By Fredricia Cunegin 57

LIVE AND LEAD YOUR LIFE UNLEASHED
By Gary Hibbs 65

THE DREAMER'S HEART
By Dr. Hermione Jourdan 73

LIVING BEYOND THE LABELS
By James Keith Powers 81

RIDE IT LIKE YOU STOLE IT!
By Judy-Ann Young 87

CASH ABUNDANCE: MORE THAN MONEY
By Katrina Fitten 95

DROWNING IN DEBT — DISCOVERING THE DREAM OF DETERMINATION
By Dr. Lorie A. L. Nicholas 101

HEED THE CALL OR PLAY IT SAFE?
By MarieYolaine Toms 109

EVERY SETBACK IS A SETUP FOR A COMEBACK
By Michelle Richburg 117

A JOURNEY BACK TO MYSELF
By Star Bobatoon, Esq 125

THE UNSEEN PATH TO PURPOSE
By Dr. Torrey Montgomery 131

Chasing 100: Expect to be Tested

By Andy Henriquez

What was I thinking? How could I have been so foolish, so naive? In a single moment, everything I'd worked for was gone. There I sat, head in my hands, overwhelmed with shame and crushed by the weight of failure.

This was supposed to be the launch of my entrepreneurial career, but it had spiraled into my biggest trial. I remember it as if it were yesterday, the moment that phone call came. A family friend, Shu Shu, as we affectionately nicknamed him—was bubbling with excitement. He had just heard about my bold leap, leaving my soul-crushing corporate job at one of the Big Four accounting firms. I had been miserable, and finally, after three and half years, I found the courage to step out in faith and pursue my goal of becoming an entrepreneur.

Shu Shu couldn't wait to discuss an opportunity he believed would catapult me into my entrepreneurial dreams. He arrived at my house, his arms full of brochures, his eyes brimming with excitement. As soon as we sat down at the breakfast table, he spread his papers out before me like a treasure map.

"Costa Rica," he said, "is the hottest new retirement destination. People are retiring there in droves, and the opportunities? They're incredible, Andy." His enthusiasm was infectious; the tone of his voice rang of opportunity.

He laid out a plan for investing in real estate: Buy a piece of land in Costa Rica, big enough for at least 20 manufactured homes. "It's simple," he said, "we buy the land, sell the homes and lease the plots. You see, we purchase these pre-manufactured homes for $7,000 each, flip them for $20,000, and we don't sell the land—just lease it. It's a continuous cash flow, Andy!" His excitement was palpable, and it was hard not to get caught up in it.

The more I mulled over it, the more excited I became. Andy Henriquez, the entrepreneur. Nah, Andy Henriquez, the international real estate mogul! I loved the sound of that. The next morning, I phoned him back, ready to dive in, "Where do we start?"

A week later, I was in Costa Rica. Everything Shu Shu had said seemed spot-on. The retirees loved it there; the land was ripe for development, and opportunities seemed abundant. "I'm in," I said without hesitation. We shook on it, met with an attorney, and I handed over my life's savings, feeling both exhilarated and terrified.

But before long, Shu Shu's weekly updates started to dwindle; phone calls went unanswered, and what started as a dream began to feel like a descent into a nightmare. My optimism faded into restless nights; my thoughts became riddled with doubt.

Finally, after weeks of trying and failing to reach him, I finally got through. "Brother, brother, I am so sorry," were Shu Shu's first words, and my heart sank to my stomach. "I lost the money." It felt the room spinning. The floor seemed to vanish under my feet. All my savings, gone. Just like that.

I hung up, overcome by a flood of self-doubt and despair. I went to lie down in a darkened room, where the dimness offered little relief from the intense shame and feeling of failure that consumed me. Was my entrepreneurial dream dead before it even began? Was I doomed to crawl back to my old job and be labeled a failure?

But then, in my darkest moment, an inner whisper cut through the silence: "Expect to be tested." It echoed, bouncing around the gloomy corners of my room, igniting a spark of hope. What if this nightmare was just a test? A brutal, painful test of my resolve to live a life beyond mediocrity?

EXPECT TO BE TESTED

That whisper was my turning point. It wasn't the end; it was the beginning. The real work started not with money or investments but within me. It was the day I truly began chasing 100—not as a goal, but as a commitment to continually evolve, no matter the setbacks.

Chasing 100 isn't about a finish line; it's about the resilience to keep moving when everything falls apart. It's about embracing the unknown, no matter how uncomfortable it is, and committing to the relentless pursuit of becoming the best version of yourself.

Years later, as I stand before audiences, sharing my journey and the lessons learned, I realize it all traces back to that moment. It wasn't just about becoming an entrepreneur; it was about transforming into someone who could weather the storm—a person unafraid to continuously push toward their highest potential.

"Chasing 100" is about never settling, never stopping. Though I lost my savings, what I gained in return far surpasses anything those funds could have provided. And for that, I'd do it all over again.

Many years later, this journey took on a whole new meaning.

On the surface, I appeared to be successful, having grown my speaking and coaching business to produce a six-figure revenue. Yet, no matter how hard I tried, I would have a few great months, but my annual earnings would end up being very similar to those of the year before. My breakthrough always seemed to be out of reach.

I knew I needed a shift but wasn't expecting to experience one when I attended what I thought was an ordinary book publishing workshop. The speaker, a man who had made his way from poverty to building a business empire worth over $100 million, began to share his journey. His story captivated everyone in the room, and I wondered, "How did he do it? How did he make such a huge transformation?" Just as these questions spun in my mind, someone in the audience raised their hand and asked what we all wanted to know: What was the secret to his success? The room fell silent, every one of us hanging on what we hoped was an answer that could possibly change our lives, too. The speaker paused; he smiled as he surveyed the room and agreed to share his secret.

He explained that most of us operate like a thermostat—automatically adjusting our efforts to maintain a set comfort level. He spoke about how this subconscious setting prevents us from reaching our full potential. Inspired by his analogy, I took this concept further in my own life, reframing it into something I could more tangibly relate to—the idea of a car's cruise control.

I realized that many of us set our life's cruise control to a "comfortable 75 mph," but to really make impactful changes and achieve our dreams, we need to push the pedal to 100. Embracing this mindset, I was able to double my revenue three years in a row, ultimately breaking into the seven-figure range.

Here are the four crucial steps that not only helped me chase and move closer to 100; they can also guide you in shifting your identity to reach your fullest potential:

1. Awareness: The first step is recognizing that you're operating at 75 on a self-set cruise control. It's crucial to understand that you might be subconsciously self-regulating—automatically slowing down or speeding up to maintain your comfort level, even if it means self-sabotaging. This awareness is what separates those who break free from limitations from those who stay stuck in stagnant circumstances.

2. Associations: To elevate from 75 to 100, you must surround yourself with individuals who are already operating at 100. Being in close proximity to those who perform at higher levels naturally elevates your own standards and behaviors. If you stay with those who are at 75 or lower, reaching 100 is nearly impossible.

3. Action: Achieving 100 requires actions that are aligned with the 100 you aspire to reach. This means deliberately stepping out of your comfort zone and embracing the uncomfortable actions and decisions that drive substantial

EXPECT TO BE TESTED

growth and improvement. It's about doing what the 100s do, not just aspiring to be like them.
4. Anchor: Finally, reaching 100 isn't a one-time effort; it requires making this new standard a habit. It's about solidifying your new behaviors so they become second nature. Consistency is key—it transforms temporary achievements into a permanent state of being and ensures that you don't fall back to your old 75 ways.

These steps became my blueprint, not just for business, but also for life. Whenever I feel stuck, I turn to these principles, reminding myself that to stop chasing 100 is to stop growing. If you've been inspired to chase your 100 but aren't sure how to start, consider this your blueprint. No more excuses—it's time to start chasing your 100.

BONUS VIDEO TUTORIAL::

For a deeper dive into how you can immediately apply these steps, scan the QR code below to watch a video tutorial. This exclusive content is designed to help you clearly understand each step and start effectively implementing each one in your life and business.

Scan the QR code above now and take the first step toward transforming your life.

Andy Henriquez

Meet Andy Henriquez, the master storyteller. After a successful career as a CPA at a Big Four firm, Andy took a bold leap of faith, transitioning from the corporate world to carve his own path in entrepreneurship. His journey from accounting to masterful storytelling has reshaped his life's work, empowering him to inspire and teach others through his unique perspective.

As the founder of the Master Storyteller Academy and the Million Dollar Storyteller Mastermind, Andy has transformed his gift for strategic storytelling, communication and connection into a powerful platform that teaches speakers, entrepreneurs and coaches how to harness the power of storytelling to captivate audiences, elevate their brand and increase revenue. His dynamic trainings and keynotes have not only lit up stages from corporate boardrooms to NASA's halls; they have also reshaped the stories of Fortune 500 leaders and executives.

Featured in the "Huffington Post," "Black Enterprise," and "Entrepreneur Magazine," Andy's compelling journey and unique insights into the art of storytelling have made him a sought-after speaker, trainer and coach. Whether he's captivating audiences

EXPECT TO BE TESTED

from the stage or helping others find their voices and cash in on their stories, Andy continues to inspire a new generation of purpose-driven entrepreneurs who recognize the transformative power of their stories.

Are you ready to cash in on your story?

Connect with Andy today to learn how to turn your story into profit. Visit www.AndyHenriquez.com to discover more and embark on your journey toward becoming a master storyteller with Andy Henriquez.

CHASING 100

You Don't Get to Define Me

By Althea Payne-Butler

I was in the eighth grade and full of hope and promise the day our school held its career day. I felt excited as I sat with two of my African-American friends, waiting for our turn to speak with the guidance counselor, whose job was to discuss with students their goals and potential. She was to help us choose our paths based on what interested us and what we were good at doing.

I was ready to rise above the negativity I'd experienced my whole life. My close family members, cousins, classmates, adults in the church, and even teachers had always tried to define me. They projected negativity onto me, saying who I was and who I wasn't. They said I was too skinny, stupid, dumb, poppy-eyed, and ugly. They said I would never amount to anything, that I was worthless. I heard these labels so frequently that I believed them.

Where I grew up, in small, rural Fauquier County, Va., everyone knew each other and their families. There was a distinct socioeconomic divide. My youth was a time of prejudices and gossipy party-line phones. Many families had no electricity or running water; well pumps, kerosene heaters, oil lamps and outhouses were common. My family had their share of this life. It was a harsh situation that I was all too familiar with.

My mother worked as a maid for several families. My father was a bricklayer and an alcoholic. His weekend tirades and abuse wreaked havoc on our family. I was tired of our weekend escapes from his craziness and prayed often for my family to be normal and happy, like the ones on TV.

Dreaming of a happier life, I was especially eager to learn what my options might be. We could hear the counselor as she advised others. We heard her encouraging our white classmates to pursue higher education, to consider becoming doctors, lawyers, teachers, nurses. The more I overheard, the more excited I became. Finally, it was my turn to speak with her.

She called not only me, but me and my friends into her office. Instead of hearing that our futures held promise, we listened as the counselor, avoiding eye contact and without engaging us or asking us about our passions, told us that we should follow the same paths as our mothers. She said that we should work as maids.

I looked at her as if she had grown a second head and thought, "You don't get to tell me what I can be."

I told her that I wanted to be a lawyer. Laughing as if I had told a joke, she said, "That's not going to happen!"

I pointed out that she had just told our classmates that they could be doctors, teachers and lawyers. I said to her: "You just told Dwayne he could be a lawyer, and he is hardly ever in school! When he is here, he is always in trouble."

She said that because we were Black, the best we could hope for was to be a file clerk in a basement, and that would be a stretch.

Her words were like tossing gasoline onto an ember. Minding my manners at 14 years old, I said nothing to her, but I was angry! I was seething with a fury so intense it felt like my very soul was ablaze. Those words punctured my soul. They put a crack in my heart and my spirit.

I carried that anger around with me well into my adulthood. I repeatedly relived that moment as I continued to endure abuse. The adults in my life had failed me. I was living in a world where I felt the abuse was normal and that I somehow deserved it.

When I finished high school, the counselor's words were still with me as I started applying for jobs and seeking a career. Her influence held up my life's progress. I refused to apply for any entry-level positions, such as file clerk, receptionist or secretary. We all know that we have to begin somewhere, and those are the jobs that get a person in the door, but I wouldn't consider them because the counselor had said that those types of jobs were our only options. I refused to allow that counselor to define my future.

Luckily for me, I had a praying grandmother in whom I could confide. We prayed often that someone would come into my life to guide me in the right direction. She may not have mentored me directly, but her prayers brought someone into my life who did. One of my mother's employers began to mentor me. She told me that I could have any career I wanted if I were willing to work hard for it. I listened to everything she said and was fully engaged in her mentorship.

Scared and standing in my own way, I signed up for a career training program instead of going to college. I was afraid of college because I still heard the voices of my past telling me that I was dumb, stupid and would fail. But I sailed through that training program like a hot knife in butter. It made me see that I was not stupid, that I was actually quite intelligent.

Shortly after, I turned to counseling (it's okay; do this for yourself), enrolled in college and earned multiple degrees; I utilized my career training skills and was hired for an executive assistant position, leading a team of other administrative assistants and skipping over the entry-level. I believe with all my heart that this was my reward from God for leaving my past trauma behind and letting him lead the way. This position led me to my dream job and changed my life forever! It opened so many doors. I no longer had financial struggles. This is a shouting-dancing moment right here!

Reflect with me for a moment. While my spirit was listing in the sea of others' words, I realized that half of those naysayers probably didn't even remember me or what they had said to me. They had moved on with their lives, if they were even still alive. We must push past the trauma, let it go or seek help to leave the turmoil behind. Hurt people hurt people. Unresolved trauma causes health issues and shortens lives. Love yourself and become the author of your own story. Write about the happy ending/goals you seek. Don't let anyone — no man, woman, mother, father, sister, brother, family member, friend, boss or stranger — define you. Set your boundaries and set yourself up for greatness.

You and God hold the power to obtain your goals. I learned a hard lesson and wasted too much time focusing on what others said about me. I stifled my life by blocking my own entry into my destined career. I was struggling financially, and life was hard as a single mother. I was in my own way. I was thinking that I was fighting back at a woman who disrupted my life, but only God knows how many others she affected with her unfounded, unacceptable opinions. I took back my power; I crushed the mindset that she had offered, and I revamped it. I stood tall in who I was, not in what someone called me. We all have that power. Some of us just have to dig through a little more of life's mess to find it.

A counselor once gave me some helpful tips that I still utilize. I will share them with you: Make a list of the top five things that are stressing you and things that may be holding you back. Then, start working through them one by one, crossing them off your list. Then, create a list of goals and start making them happen. Be authentically you, with life and purpose, unapologetically. You got this!

YOU DON'T GET TO DEFINE ME

Althea Payne-Butler

A distinguished engineer, author, speaker, and AI consultant with a deeply personal journey of inspiration and creativity, Althea Payne-Butler is the founder of SOWEGO Enterprises and Victory Chronicles. Her greatest achievement in life has been her children and grandchildren. With over two decades of expertise in government contracting, she excels in information technology and program management. Althea holds an MBA and an MS in information technology management.

Beyond her professional achievements, Althea has never met a stranger. Her personal life is a rich tapestry of love, resilience, and creativity. Althea has been a mother, sister, and auntie figure to many. In fact, her husband, James, calls her the "Baby Whisperer." Everywhere she goes, with a warm heart and smile, she attracts children and new friends.

Althea's nurturing spirit is recognized among her friends and family and extends to her writing. Her book, "Fragmented Heart," made #1 on Amazon's Top Hot New Releases list and was among the top 100 journals on Amazon. "Fragmented Heart" reveals her journey through life's challenges and her unwavering *spirit of learning and overcoming. It contains a collection of short stories and activities that will help the reader reflect, relax, and promote healing.*

Althea stands as a testament to the power of balancing a demanding professional life with personal passions. Her journey inspires many to pursue excellence in their careers while nurturing their creative and personal growth, making her a true example of inspiration and strength.

You may contact Althea at Althea.a.payne@gmail.com.

I Had a Daddy All Along

By Angeleen Harris

I stand at the kitchen window, my hands submerged in soapy water as I scrub the dinner dishes. The scent of my mother's famous gumbo still lingers in the air, a bittersweet reminder of happier times when our family was whole. But now, at 13, I'm the one stirring the pot, trying to fill the void left by a father who's no longer here.

The screen door slams open, and my little sister Nessa bursts in, her face streaked with tears and her breath coming in ragged gasps. "Angie! He took my ball! He hit me!" she wails, collapsing against me.

Something inside me snaps. The weight of being the oldest, the protector, the stand-in parent, crashes down on my narrow shoulders. I grab the butcher knife from the counter, its weight unfamiliar and terrifying in my hand. As I storm out onto our sunbaked street, ready to confront Nessa's tormentor, a single thought pounds through my head: Where are you, Daddy? We need you.

But the bully is gone, leaving only the echo of Nessa's sobs and the bitter taste of helplessness in my mouth. That night, as I lie in bed, my mind races with plans for revenge, desperate schemes to protect my family. It's then that the cruel reality hits me like a physical blow: I am alone in this. My father, my protector, is gone.

This moment of revelation etches itself into my soul, a defining crossroads where childhood innocence collides head-on with the harsh realities of a broken home.

Years pass, but the weight of that day never fully lifts. I carry it with me like a shadow, coloring my relationships and my sense of self-worth. The absence of paternal protection becomes a lens through which I view the world – a world where trust is fragile, where love can disappear, where I must always be on guard.

There are nights when I wake in a cold sweat, the old anger and fear bubbling up from some deep, hidden well. I feel the phantom weight of that kitchen knife in my hand, and my heart aches with a cocktail of emotions: rage at the injustice, sorrow for the little girl I was, and a gnawing, persistent longing for the father who should have been there.

But as I chase my full potential, striving toward that elusive "100" in life and business, I begin to unravel the tangled knot of my past. Slowly, painfully, I learn to see beyond the hurt little girl's perspective. I realize that my father's absence, while profoundly impactful, doesn't define me. It has shaped me, yes, but it doesn't have to limit me.

From this journey, I've gleaned three powerful lessons:

1. ***Resilience is born from adversity.***
That day with the knife taught me that I have an inner strength I never knew existed. While I shouldn't have had to be so strong so young, that resilience has served me well throughout my life.

2. ***Our perceptions shape our reality.***
For years, I believed my father's absence meant he didn't care. But as I've grown, I've learned that people's actions — or inactions — are often more complex than we realize as children. Understanding this has allowed me to heal and approach relationships with more empathy and nuance.

3. ***We have the power to rewrite our stories.***
While I can't change the past, I can choose how I let it affect my present and future. By actively working to release the pain and resentment, I'm freeing myself to pursue my full potential.

I HAD A DADDY ALL ALONG

As I stand here today, a successful woman chasing her dreams, I realize a profound truth: My father does love me, in his own way. His absence, while painful, doesn't negate the love he expressed when he was present. This understanding doesn't erase the past, but it allows me to move forward with a lighter heart.

To those who carry similar wounds, I say this: Your past does not define your future. Every day is an opportunity to take a step towards your full potential, to release the anchors of past hurt, and embrace the possibilities that lie ahead. Start by acknowledging your pain, but don't let it be the end of your story. Seek understanding, practice forgiveness — of others and yourself — and set your sights on the incredible future you deserve.

Remember, chasing 100 isn't about perfection; it's about progress. It's about consistently moving forward, even when the path is unclear. It's about transforming your life by releasing the past that holds you back and refusing to settle for mediocrity. There is always another level of accomplishment waiting for you, another goal to strive for, another milestone to reach.

So today, I challenge you: Take one small step toward healing an old wound. Reach out to someone you've been avoiding; write a letter you never intended to send, or simply look in the mirror and tell yourself, "I am worthy of love and success." Because you are. We all are. And it's time we started believing it.

In the end, I've learned that while I may have grown up feeling fatherless, I was never truly alone. The strength I thought I lacked was within me all along. And now, as I continue chasing my 100, I carry that strength with pride, knowing that every challenge I overcome is a testament to the resilient spirit that was forged in the crucible of my childhood.

So, here's to the journey ahead, to the heights we've yet to reach, and to the incredible potential that lies within each of us. Let's chase it together, unapologetically and with open hearts. After all, our greatest victories are often born from our deepest struggles. And in that truth, I find both solace and boundless hope for the future.

Angeleen Harris

Angeleen Harris is a strong advocate of the financial success of Black businesswomen. Throughout her career, she has been committed to the cause of empowering women entrepreneurs to grow, flourish and thrive by improving their cash flow, enhancing net profits, and reducing taxes so that they keep more of their hard-earned money in the bank. Her rallying cry has always been, "Financial literacy and strategic planning are key tools to success." Angeleen is dedicated to providing women with the leadership, resources and support they need to overcome the challenges of entrepreneurship.

The most important thing for her is the empowerment of Black women, equipping them with the confidence and tools to take control of their financial futures and build lasting wealth. She believes that by fostering financial independence, Black women can not only transform their own lives but also uplift their communities. Her work is driven by a deep passion for seeing women succeed, and she continuously strives to create a world where every Black woman can achieve her dreams and thrive in business.

I HAD A DADDY ALL ALONG

Angeleen's commitment goes beyond just financial growth; it's about creating sustainable success and ensuring that Black women have the resources and knowledge they need to navigate the complexities of entrepreneurship. She is unwavering in her mission to help women unlock their full potential and create legacies of wealth and success that will endure for generations.

You may reach Angeleen at contactus@growthriveprospercollective.com.

CHASING 100

ALL STEPS ARE MIGHTY!

By Brian H. Nicholas, LAc

The Smart One:

When I was growing up, my family and my teachers constantly told me how smart I was. In the beginning, I believed it. My grades were a testament to that, and I carried the identity of "the smart one" with pride. But as I moved through school, things started to change. My grades slipped from As to Bs and even Cs. At first I convinced myself that it was a passing thing. However, eventually, I couldn't avoid that scoring Bs, Cs and Ds had become the new normal for me. I didn't understand why. I was doing the same thing as before; why had my grades gone down? The shame I felt about my grades grew with every academic year. I felt like I wasn't living up to the expectations that I had set. We used to joke whenever I'd make even a B. Now that joking was replaced with silently passing my report card to my mom, avoiding any conversation and accepting the trouble I'd be in when my father came home. The more my grades slipped, the more I felt like I was losing a part of myself. The identity I had clung to slipped through my fingers. I told myself that things would change, but I didn't know what to do to change them.

Walking the Dog:

We had a strict rule at home: School clothes were for school, and house clothes were for everything else. Unfortunately for me, my house clothes included high-water pants – and no, not nearly as high as those the nerdy character Steve Urkel wore on the show "Family Matters," but that didn't matter – they were high enough to draw ridicule. But after school, I'd change into my house clothes and walk the dog, always dreading the inevitable moment when I'd have to clean up after him in front of a group of kids who never missed a chance to snicker at my high-water pants.

Those walks were a daily humiliation. I prayed for rain and was happier when the weather turned too cold for those youngsters to hang out outside. I was happy for anything that would help me avoid those stares and whispers. It wasn't just the clothes or the teasing that bothered me, though. It was a deeper feeling of not fitting in—whether in the neighborhood, where I wasn't athletic or outgoing; or even at church, where I felt like an outsider, since we traveled to church from Brooklyn.

The isolation was weary. I couldn't escape the feeling that I was always on the outside looking in, searching for where I belonged. That sense of not fitting in, of being different, stayed with me for years, shaping how I saw myself and how I navigated the world.

The TV:

As a young Black boy, I saw TV shows and listened to news that fed me a steady diet of negative portrayals of people who looked like me. I saw Black men depicted as drug dealers, pimps, and the like. I rarely saw Black people portrayed as municipal workers, professionals or business owners like the men and women in my family or in my community whom my father and mother introduced us to. The Black characters were hardly ever part of or leaders of organizations that were doing positive things to make a difference.

Most nights the news showed images of a young Black man with his head down, handcuffs showing, and the police taking him either into a police station or into a squad car. That was the most common image that I saw of young Black men on the news, regardless of the channel delivering the reports.

My mother, trying to protect me, would constantly warn, "Don't be like those boys." But what neither she nor I understood was that what I saw on the screen and heard at home seeped into my subconscious, shaping how I viewed myself. I began to internalize those images and the poisonous messages they carried, believing that my potential was limited, and that the world saw me as nothing more than a problem, a nuisance at best and a criminal at worst. This constant reinforcement of negative stereotypes weighed heavily on me, leading to a sense of hopelessness that had no voice. I felt like I was walking through a life, where others had preconceived notions of who I was and what my potential was, while I silently suffered under the weight without understanding why.

The Job Line Revelation:

At the end of high school, I needed money for college, so I set out to find a job. I spotted a classified ad for a fast-food position and arrived early to apply, thinking I'd beat the crowd. But when I got there, I was stunned. A line of young Black and Latino men stretched around the block, all hoping for the same job. As I walked down that line, reality hit me hard.

The conversations I overheard broke my heart. Young men just like me were talking about how this job would be their last chance before they'd have to join the military. They all said they'd been turned away from countless other jobs – there were more young men than jobs.

These were not the young men I saw on TV, men portrayed as criminals or troublemakers. These were young men just like me, trying to support themselves and their families. It was a gut-wrenching moment that shattered the narrative I had unknowingly absorbed from the media. The anger and frustration I felt were overwhelming. I had been lied to my entire life, made to believe a version of reality that wasn't true. From that day forward, I refused to accept those negative images and false narratives.

I realized that while I didn't know how to change what the

media presented, I could begin to shift the false narratives I had accepted about myself and other young Black men – it served me well when it came time for me to raise sons and participate in youth programs.

The Soul-Restorative Revelation:

Years later, after college, I was working as a corporate technical trainer. During this time, I stumbled upon a lecture series in Harlem that featured prominent Black scholars like Dr. John Henrik Clarke and Dr. Yosef Ben-Jochannan. Walking into the church where the lecture series was held, I felt for the first time like I was coming home. The atmosphere was alive with knowledge, a respect and love for culture and a deep sense of community. It was the complete opposite of the shame and disempowerment I had felt all those years ago in elementary school when learning about Black history solely through the lens of slavery.

This experience was soul-restorative, and it would take me on a journey of healing the wounds that years of miseducation had inflicted. It gave me a new perspective on my heritage, one filled with pride and empowerment, backed up by knowledge. This revelation was a turning point that helped me reclaim my identity and inspired me to pursue a path where I could contribute to uplifting and educating others in my community.

Conclusion: Chasing 100 –
Embracing the Power of Each Step

As I reflect on my journey, it's clear that the revelations I've had were more than just moments of clarity; they were life-altering turning points that reshaped my understanding of myself and the world around me. The job-line experience opened my eyes to the pervasive falsehoods that society often imposes on young Black men like me, while the Harlem lectures reconnected me with a legacy of greatness that had been systematically hidden from us. These moments taught me the power of narrative and how crucial it is to take control of the stories we tell ourselves and others.

ALL STEPS ARE MIGHTY!

Now, as I'm "Chasing 100," striving to become the best version of myself, I realize that this journey isn't about perfection—it's about progress. It's about recognizing that every step, no matter how small, holds immense power. Each decision, each thought, and each action contribute to the narrative we build for our lives. And just like an atom, seemingly insignificant on its own, each step has the potential to create tremendous impact.

I've learned that I can, and we can focus on what we can create now. It's easy to get bogged down by past failures or missed opportunities, but true power lies in our ability to take the next step forward. Whether it's a tiny action or a monumental decision, what matters is the intention and the direction in which we move.

I invite you to embrace this mindset as well. Understand that your power lies in the steps you take—those that align with your truth, your purpose and your vision for a better self. Acknowledge that these gifts of purpose and vision come to us from the Divine in each of us. Celebrate each step with gratitude, recognizing the Divine wisdom, guidance and love that accompany you on your journey. By doing so, you can begin to rewrite your own story, breaking free from the narratives that have held you back and stepping into a life of authenticity and fulfillment.

In the end, chasing 100 isn't just about reaching a destination; it's about the journey itself. It's about honoring each step you take, knowing that every single one brings you closer to the empowered, authentic version of yourself that you were always meant to be. So, keep moving forward, one step at a time, and watch as your story unfolds in ways you never imagined possible.

Brian H. Nicholas, LAc

Brian H. Nicholas, LAc., is a passionate healer and transformational coach dedicated to guiding individuals toward profound healing and empowerment. With a deep commitment to blending ancient wisdom and modern science, Brian specializes in liberating his clients from the energetic burdens of chronic pain, trauma, and stress. Through his integrative approach, which includes Emotional Freedom Technique (EFT), pranic healing, NLP, and HeartMath techniques, Brian helps individuals reconnect with their innate strengths and rediscover their potential.

Brian's work is driven by a profound belief in the power of energy healing and mindset transformation to create lasting change. He is devoted to helping his clients break free from the past, heal on all levels—physically, mentally, and emotionally—and step into a life of fulfillment and inner peace.

Connect with Brian to embark on a journey of healing and transformation, where every step leads you closer to a more Divinely inspired, empowered and authentic self.

Instagram: @thedesignedtotransform
Phone: 862.201.3530

When Enough Became Everything

By Charese L. Josie

I was supposed to go to college. I was supposed to get a good job, and I was supposed to get married. But what I was meant to do was chase my dream and live my own life.

It was 11 p.m., and the silence in my apartment was deafening. I got out of bed, my heart pounding, and I walked to the dresser. Each step was heavy with the unavoidable decision. When I reached the dresser, I hesitated, a tightness gripping my chest. Deep down, I knew a decision was right in front of me—one I could no longer avoid.

The flickering television cast a faint light across the room as I stared into the mirror. The stillness around me amplified the chaos inside. I took deep breaths as I finally summoned the courage to ask the question that had haunted me for three years: "What are you fighting for?"

As the youngest and only daughter, I carried the weight of societal and familial expectations. My parents never explicitly pressured me, but the path was laid out—college, a good job, marriage. Their words, "Your brother will go into the military, and you will go to college, get a good job and get married one day," shaped my future. The self-induced pressure to conform to these expectations was immense.

After six years of college, I had everything—except the one thing that seemed to matter most. The degrees were framed on the wall, and the career was on track, but the absence of marriage gnawed at me. Disappointment settled in, a quiet ache I tried to bury beneath my professional achievements. I moved four hours away, started my first salaried job and kept in touch with a man I'd met just before the move. We dated long distance, and when we married a year and a half later, it felt like the final box was checked.

At 26, I married, but doubts had already taken root. "I'm not sure how this is going to work, but you've figured everything else out—you'll do it this time, too," I told myself. I quit my job, packed up my life and moved four hours away again, believing adults did this when they married. But deep down, the unease never left.

Being the responsible child shaped me into a perfectionist, yet I often felt misunderstood. People saw the surface but never the struggle underneath. They assumed I had it all together, that I was confident and capable when, in reality, I was wrestling with self-doubt and fear of failure. This misunderstanding added to the pressure, making me feel isolated. No matter what I did, no one could see the real me—the one trying to hold everything together.

The anxiety gripped me as soon as I pulled into my new apartment complex. My breathing quickened, and the short drive to the back felt endless. Even walking up the stairs to the second floor seemed to take forever. I can still remember the weight of the key in my hand and how it felt as I turned it in the lock. Every time, I hesitated, unsure of what I would find on the other side of that door. Would he be in the same spot on the floor, engrossed in video games, showing no interest in helping to set up our new life? Would I be greeted with a simple "hey" without warmth or eye contact?

As I stepped inside, I fought to keep my frustration in check. I didn't want to be the nagging wife, continually picking at the seams of our marriage. I had to get this right. As I went to the bedroom, I casually asked about hanging up pictures. Once again, I was reminded of the stress and pressure I was under, and the acne on my face was not helpful. It seemed strange to have breakouts at this point in my life, but I brushed it off as a byproduct of stress, lack of sleep and some peculiar season of growth. I never stopped to consider that it might be more than that—that it might be my marriage, or perhaps even more troubling, that it was me not fighting for myself.

One night, my husband was out late again, as usual. The phone rang at 11 p.m., and a woman on the other end told me she was with him. Anger surged within me, and I considered every possible reaction—getting dressed, confronting him, screaming, breaking things. But at that moment, I realized that none of these actions would change anything; they would only deplete me further. After years of carrying this stress, I knew that if anything was going to change, it had to start with me. And then it dawned on me—this wasn't just a failure. I was failing. I was failing to fight for myself, to demand the respect and love I deserved. After three years of relentless stress, I just wanted peace. This was my moment of realization, my moment of power. It was the moment I realized that I had the power to change my life, to fight for myself.

I got out of bed, stood in front of the mirror in my bedroom, took a deep breath and faced the question that had been tormenting me: "What are you fighting for?" The answers were clear: to avoid the shame of failing at a significant life event, to maintain the facade of having it all together and to meet the societal expectation of a successful marriage. But I realized they weren't enough—I wasn't fighting for myself. That night, at 11 p.m., I made a choice. I chose to fight for myself. As I gazed into my eyes, I felt the stress and tension leave my body, like a knot slowly loosening its grip. It was as if I could breathe fully for the first time in years.

After months of my asking him to, he finally moved out. The next day, I instinctively waited for the familiar wave of anxiety. But instead, I was met with an unfamiliar stillness, a quiet that felt foreign yet comforting. I peeked out the window, and for the first time in years, the sunlight didn't seem harsh—it was warm, inviting and full of promise. I took a deep breath, feeling the weight lift as I realized I hadn't slept in three years. The relief was profound.

It wasn't about him or even the relationship. At that moment,

CHASING 100

I realized the lengths I had gone to fight for everything except myself. Standing there at 28 years old, I didn't know if I would ever have children or get married again. But I knew it wasn't enough to stay in a place that depleted me. That's where my courage began, and my confidence grew in a way I never imagined. I learned to embrace the unknown, understanding that this was a crucial step from merely getting by to thriving. I realized I could live a fulfilling life, even if it meant being single, because I was not alone. Though I didn't know if I would ever become a parent, I knew I had a lot of love to give, and that was enough for me.

Courage and confidence were born when he moved out, and each step I took strengthened my confidence, showing me that I was capable of more than I ever imagined.

One of the critical lessons I learned was the importance of examining why I felt the way I did. I began to see paths to happiness that didn't rely on the things I once thought were essential. I recognized the unrealistic expectations I had placed on myself and understood that I was more in charge of my happiness than I had allowed myself to believe. I reclaimed calmness and strength—two things I feared I was losing. These lessons didn't change me at only that moment—they continue to guide me today, reminding me that my happiness is within my control and that my true strength lies in choosing what suits me.

Since then, I no longer make decisions or take on tasks to prove that I can. Looking back, the dissolution of the marriage was not a surprise—it was realizing how much time and energy I had spent trying to make something work that wasn't right for me.

Today, I am remarried. I have two beautiful daughters, a stress-free job and a thriving business. But more importantly, I've found peace in living a life that's mine—a life where I chase my dreams, not the ones laid out for me. The weight of expectations has been replaced by a strength born from choosing myself.

I was supposed to go to college. I was supposed to get a job. I was supposed to get married. But what I was supposed to do was chase my dream and live my own life—and that's precisely what I've done.

Charese L. Josie

For decades, Charese Josie battled with the silent struggle many high-achieving individuals face—measuring self-worth by achievements alone. This relentless pursuit of success became her mile markers, leaving her disconnected from meaningful relationships, especially with herself. While she achieved remarkable career success, she faced significant challenges in her personal and professional life. When these worlds collided, Charese made a bold decision: to step into discomfort and rebuild her confidence and judgment from the ground up. Her journey is a testament to the transformative power of self-awareness and the possibility of personal and professional growth.

Through this journey, Charese committed to understanding her strengths and challenges, using this awareness to guide her decisions and actions. She strives for consistency, ensuring that she remains true to her values no matter the environment. Charese learned that to lead at the highest level, she must first take responsibility for herself. She is passionate about helping others do the same—because when we care for ourselves, we not only create the life we desire but also empower ourselves to lead effectively.

Today, Charese works with high-achieving leaders who feel they've done all the "right" things but aren't getting the results they want. She teaches early to mid-level leaders how to boost their decision-making confidence and excel in their roles, empowering them to create the work-life balance they've been striving for, reducing overwhelm and anxiety.

Visit www.charesejosie.com to learn more about Charese and her services.

Embracing My True Reflection

By Darlene L. Thorne, MDiv

Too black. Preacher's kid. Too proper. Most likely to succeed? Uh, no. I attempted suicide at the age of 15. But what I did not realize is that there was more at stake than my color, my family background or how I spoke. I had the lives of so many others in my hands, and if I did not complete my mission, what would happen to the ones I did not reach? I had to live. There was no other option. The question was, though… who was I?

It took a serendipitous moment, a chance encounter with a legend, for me to understand the answer to that. But before this encounter, I had struggled with serious self-image issues.

My parents were the pastors of a prominent church in New Jersey, and my father was also a substitute teacher in the local school district. He also ran the high school suspension program at our church. Any suspended student would come to our church for class. Our family and a few others were among the first to integrate an elementary school in the city of Linden, N.J. I had no idea that we were making history, but my experience from first through sixth grade was good. I had no idea what would await me in junior high school.

In junior high, the other students taunted me and talked about me because I was different. I dreaded going to school. The junior high school was already integrated, and we took the bus to and from school. I hated it. Every day others teased me, took my lunch money and subjected me to outrageous threats and bullying. The girls and boys who teased me were from "the other side of the tracks," meaning that I was from the so-called "rich" side of the tracks. My parents taught me not to fight, not to bad mouth people. I did not know how to defend myself, so I tried to blend in, but it didn't work. I wasn't accepted because they knew I was trying to be someone I was not.

Back then, I wore a lot of navy, dark brown and black, thinking those colors would hide me, make me invisible. But my efforts did not keep Janet (not her real name) from threatening to beat me up after school every day. It did not keep my so-called friends who went to church with me on Sunday from talking about me on Monday. I told my mom and dad how awful it was, and my mom repeated the old adage: "Sticks and stones may break your bones, but words will never hurt you." Words were hurting me.

I felt like such an outsider. I was 14 and felt so different from even my siblings, I asked my mother if I had been adopted. And now things were worse.

I was literally dying inside. I had gotten so sick that I was not eliminating — I was not having bowel movements. My stomach had become rock hard, and I had to have a diet of prune juice and mineral oil for weeks to get my body to cooperate.

Amid my turmoil at school, I faced a heartbreaking blow. My parents divorced. I was 15 when my family—without my dad—moved away. My dad, my rock, the one who really understood me, was gone. He was the one who knew about how bad the teasing made me feel—he "got" me. We bore the same complexion, and he understood my pain. I could go to him when I felt bad, and he would comfort me. But now he was gone, and I felt so alone. I just wanted to die.

My mother didn't understand what I was going through, and now my dad was gone. It seemed like an eternity passed before I heard from him. I told him I wanted to live with him. Being an immature 15-year-old, I told him I hated where we were living and that nobody understood me except him. He told me that he was not in a position for me to come live with him. I felt rejected and abandoned. I decided I need to take an extended nap. I took a bottle of my mother's pills (honestly, I never figured out what they were) and downed them with some aspirin. I fell asleep, and hours later, my sister awakened me. I was so angry, but the failed suicide attempt made an impact on me. I thought that maybe God would not let me die and that possibly being in a different place might prove to be something worthwhile.

In our new location, while I didn't have my dad, I also didn't have the teasing or bullying. There were 1,000 students in the high school, and my graduating class size was 274. I was one of five brown students in the entire school. There was more intrigue and interest in me because I was different. Life began fresh for me, and I had such a better outlook on life that I even decided I would go to college. I applied and was accepted to Northeastern University in Boston, Massachusetts.

And while life was better, I still viewed myself critically. That was about to change. The spring of my freshman year, my friend and I were walking in Harvard Square when we literally ran into the famous actor Sidney Poitier, who was filming a movie. We said hello and walked a few feet then stopped and turned to each other, screaming his name! We ran back to catch up with him, and we chatted for just a few minutes. But before we left, he looked into my eyes, took my hands in his, and he said, "You are a beautiful Black woman!" Those words changed my life.

All of the hurt from past aggressions disappeared. To think that someone I admired from afar saw something in me! This hit me in my core. From that day on, I saw myself in an entirely different light. Sidney Poitier saw something in me that I had never seen nor felt!

My belief system changed. I felt my confidence increase—I was meditating, as though it were, on the words that Mr. Poitier spoke to me. Every time I looked in the mirror, I saw a new me. I began to say, "I am a beautiful Black woman!" I smiled more. The changes were small at first, but as T. Harv Eker said, "What you focus on expands. Where attention flows, energy flows, and results will show."

What were the results that began to show? Instead of following in the shadows to be hidden, I started the journey of discovering who I am and why I was created. I became the very best version of myself. I changed my major to communications and focused on what my prayers revealed I was created to do: to make an impact on the world by sharing my story to influence and help other women transform.

I had come to realize is that there is no one else in this world who can do what I do the way I do it. I did not need to compare myself to anyone. I am to run my own race and manifest the destiny for which I was created. "The greatest discovery in life is self-discovery. Until you find yourself, you will always be someone else. Become yourself."— Myles Munroe

When I changed the way I thought about me, I changed the way I showed up to the world. My potential began to appear. The thing you think about most is what you will manifest.

When I thought about who I was not, I produced at a low level. However, when I changed what I thought about me, I began to see even negative things in a positive light. I had the fuel to push harder. When I started showing up as the real me, I learned to really love me! The people I get to serve are amazing! If I had not decided to change the way I thought about myself and if I had not taken the proper steps to become the authentic me, what I do now would have never materialized.

I recall meeting some new members at church. I met the parents and then was introduced to their beautiful chocolate drop of a daughter, Jordi. She looked like me, and I remember taking her hands and looking into her dark eyes and telling her, "You are a beautiful young lady!"

Years later her mother told me that the day I spoke those words to her daughter, it changed her young life. She had been experiencing issues with self-acceptance for her deep skin color. She went on to graduate from high school, becoming Miss Jabberwocky (this is a tradition of Delta Sigma Theta Sorority Inc. This event involves young women engaging in social, cultural and service activities. It serves as a platform for personal development and community involvement, often culminating in a scholarship program where participants raise funds for educational purposes), earning a college scholarship. She became a law enforcement agent and in more recent years has gotten married and has a beautiful baby boy.

I can now confidently answer the question, "Who am I?" I am a beautiful Black woman who is changing lives!

Darlene Thorne, MDiv

Pastor Darlene Thorne, MDiv, is a multifaceted leader, devoted wife, mother, author, speaker, coach and mentor. Her life is deeply rooted in faith, family and community. Darlene's journey began with singing in church alongside her sisters, igniting a lifelong passion for music and worship. At 18, she fully dedicated her life to Christ, beginning her ministry.

Darlene and her husband, Pastor Kevin Thorne, lead Renewal Community Church in Clayton, N.C. They are proud parents of two accomplished young adults, Kevin II and Kennedy Elayne.

As CEO of A Heart After the Father LLC, Darlene guides women caregivers in holistic self-care. She developed the Refresh, Refill, and Renew framework, which empowers women to prioritize self-care and overcome guilt, enabling them to thrive in all areas of life. Her coaching focuses on helping caregiving entrepreneurs establish sustainable self-care routines.

An international speaker, Darlene shares impactful messages at conferences and workshops worldwide, emphasizing personal growth, spiritual development, and life balance. Her influence extends beyond the pulpit through active community engagement. An accomplished international speaker, Darlene has delivered powerful messages at numerous conferences and workshops, reaching audiences around the globe. Her teachings focus on personal growth, spiritual development and the importance of maintaining a healthy balance in life. Darlene actively engages with her community and followers through various platforms.

Darlene Thorne continues to inspire others with her dedication to faith and self-care. Connect with her at linktr.ee/Ladydarlene.

CHASING 100

Wearing a Mask of Strength

By Dashana Jefferies

Beneath the Moon

I was in a fetal position, expecting not to wake up. I was bound to my bed, unable to move my body, my legs, my arms. The pain was unbearable, and the weight of my depression had crushed every bit of hope I had left. I had reached my breaking point. The pills and alcohol were supposed to numb everything, to end the torment. I was ready to let go, to end the pain that had consumed my life.

Every breath felt like a burden, each heartbeat a reminder of the unbearable pain that had become my constant companion. I was drowning in a sea of despair, feeling utterly alone and convinced that the only way out was to let go forever. The isolation was suffocating, and the relentless ache in my heart from betrayal made every moment agonizing. I wanted to escape the darkness that had swallowed my soul, and in that moment, I truly believed there was no other way to find peace.

Grappling Shadows

Despair had been lurking in the shadows of my life for as long as I could remember, but I had always managed to push it back. This time, though, it had dug deep into my soul. The feeling of worthlessness became all-encompassing. Every aspect of my life felt like a failure—relationships, career, even my role as a friend. Moments of betrayal from someone I loved overshadowed everything good in my life, making me question my existence.

Being strong exhausted me. The energy I had to survive was empty. I hated being called resilient. I didn't want to be known anymore for being able to take hit after hit. I needed someone to hold me, someone to take the weight off my shoulders, someone else to be the strong one.

The Revelation

A tiny flicker of resolve broke through the overwhelming despair as I lay there, waiting for the darkness to take over. It was as if, in the depths of my anguish, a whisper of hope managed to pierce through the suffocating weight of my depression. I made a promise to God—a desperate bargain with the universe. If I survived this night, I vowed I would seek help. There was more to this than a plea for mercy. It was a recognition that I deserved a chance to heal, to live, to find a way out of this endless torment, but only if it wasn't my time.

That night, something profound happened. I did die—not physically, but mentally and spiritually. The person I was up until that point ceased to exist. The broken, exhausted version of myself, who had carried the burden of unrelenting sadness and relentless anxiety, began to fade away. In that moment of utter surrender, a new sense of purpose emerged. As a fragile yet powerful spark, this flicker of resolve was my lifeline that God refused to extinguish.

The Impact

Keeping my promise to God and myself, I immediately sought therapy. I was determined to honor the commitment I had made to myself. The first sessions were terrifying; I had to lay bare my soul and confront the very demons I had tried to silence. But I knew it was the only way forward.

Through therapy, I was diagnosed with clinical depression. I learned that clinical depression is more than just feeling sad. It's a persistent emptiness and hopelessness that doesn't go away. Looking back, I realized these feelings had been with me

WEARING A MASK OF STRENGTH

for most of my life. I had masked them by being a firm friend, always there for others but never for myself. The weight of this constant darkness had finally become too much to bear.

I was also diagnosed with PTSD, a result of relational trauma. The betrayal I experienced was a trigger but not the sole cause. Therapy helped me see that my PTSD was rooted in past relationships and friendships where I had felt used and betrayed. These experiences left deep scars that I had never allowed to heal. Acknowledging this trauma was a painful yet necessary step toward recovery.

Another diagnosis that emerged was anxiety. My anxiety was a constant state of fear and apprehension that had been crippling my daily life. Therapy helped me trace its roots back to my childhood and my role as a caretaker. I was always trying to fix others while neglecting myself. This realization was a turning point in my therapy, helping me to understand why I felt the way I did and how to start addressing it.

The mask of strength can hide the deepest wounds. For years, I had portrayed myself as strong and capable, but I was falling apart. The events leading up to my suicide attempt were the culmination of years of neglecting my own needs and feelings. The betrayal of fake love was the final straw, but it was also the catalyst for my healing journey.

The Journey to Recovery

Therapy was just the beginning. It helped me understand my diagnosis and look back at my life through a new lens. It was the start of my path to recovery, and while the journey has been long and hard, it's also been gratifying. I began to rebuild my life step by step. I found a new purpose and direction, turning my pain into a mission to help others. My experiences became the foundation for my work in mental health advocacy and education. I created A Passport 2 Breathe, an app to support those with mental struggles, and wrote books to inspire and uplift others.

Today, I am a million-dollar, international award-winning speaker and author who educates the world on mental health.

By sharing my story on global stages and through my writing, I aim to break down the stigma surrounding mental health and provide hope and practical tools for struggling people. My journey from despair to empowerment has not only transformed my life but has also given me the platform to impact countless others, showing them that there is always a way forward.

Lesson Learned

One of the most profound insights I've gained is the transformative power of vulnerability. Admitting that you're struggling is not a sign of weakness; it's an act of courage. It's in those moments of honesty with ourselves and others that true healing begins. Seeking help isn't about surrendering but reclaiming your strength and taking proactive steps toward recovery.

Healing is a journey, often winding and unpredictable. There will be setbacks and triumphs, but each step forward is a victory. Embrace the support of your friends, family, therapists, and communities. They are your anchors in the storm, offering stability when needed.

Rising Again

If you've made it this far, you've already taken a step toward your healing journey. My story isn't just about surviving—it's about finding the strength to redefine my life in the aftermath of despair. It's about the gritty, raw rebuilding process when everything feels broken. I've learned that the pieces we pick up and the scars we bear make us beautifully human.

You might feel lost or overwhelmed right now, and that's okay. In these moments of uncertainty, we discover who we indeed are. Don't be afraid to ask for help, to lean on others and to let yourself be vulnerable. There's immense power in admitting that you can't do it alone. I didn't become more robust by pretending to be invincible; I found my strength by embracing my fragility and seeking support.

Think of your life as a canvas. The dark strokes are part of your story but don't define the entire picture. You have the

WEARING A MASK OF STRENGTH

brush in your hand and the ability to add colors, textures and depth to your narrative. Therapy, community and self-compassion are your tools.

So, here's my challenge to you:
1. Start painting what your new life could be like.
2. Reach out for help; explore therapy and connect with others who understand.
3. Allow yourself the freedom to be imperfect, to heal at your own pace. Your journey won't look like anyone else's, and that's what makes it uniquely yours.

Take this story as a reminder that no matter how deep the darkness is, there is always a flicker of light waiting to guide you back. You are not alone in this; together, we can rise, heal, and thrive.

Dashana Jefferies

Meet Dashana Jefferies, a Million-Dollar Storyteller, award-winning speaker, author and CEO of the acclaimed AI consulting firm, Passport 2 Breathe. Her transformative journey from deep despair to inspiring resilience has reshaped her life and empowered others to navigate their storms with courage.

Having earned bachelor's and master's degrees in psychology and being certified in mental health first aid, Dashana has a profound commitment to mental wellness. In response to the urgent need for accessible mental health support, she created the Passport 2 Breathe app, a vital resource offering motivation, meditation and support to those facing mental health challenges.

Recognizing the specific needs of individuals with ADD or ADHD, she also developed a tailored Chat GPT tool to simplify academic tasks and enhance time management, acting as a virtual mentor. This innovation stemmed from Dashana's battle with clinical depression, anxiety and PTSD in 2019, a crisis that ignited her determination to foster hope and healing for others.

Dashana is also the author of "365 Intentional Breaths" and "365 Love Letters to the World's Black Kings," books that offer daily affirmations and support and celebrate the strength and resilience of the human spirit. Her work exemplifies the power of vulnerability and the importance of community in overcoming adversity. Dashana invites everyone to join her on a journey of healing and thriving, one intentional breath at a time.

Reach Dashana: Customerservice@apassport2breathe.com.

CHASING 100

You Are Not Them

By Elaine Robinson Beattie

Sitting in my favorite stylish suite at the Loews New York Hotel in Midtown Manhattan, a symbol of the success I had worked so hard to attain, I felt a sense of accomplishment. My mother, visiting with a friend, joined me on this rare occasion. As we discussed my career, she looked at me with tears in her eyes. Her words that still echo in my mind: "One day, you're going to wake up, and I pray you will not be devastated. You are not them. The rules of the game are different for you."

I was confused. I had achieved so much—a successful career, a high-ranking position and the respect of my peers. But my mother, who had seen me work 10-, 12-, even 14-hour days for over a decade, was heartbroken and frightened for me. Despite my hard work and qualifications, she witnessed the countless times I had been passed over for better promotions. She was heartbroken for me that I had bought into the lie—that if I got a good education, worked hard, had faith and stayed out of trouble, I could achieve the American Dream.

I refused to remove my rose-colored glasses. I believed that my hard work and determination would eventually pay off. But my mother was not convinced. She remembered my phone call to her, early in my career, when I expressed sheer excitement. I had been invited to Boston to interview for a management trainee position with Sheraton Hotels, and I told her how proud I was when they offered me the position on the spot. I was going to be a general manager in 10 years!

However, she also remembered the call I made to her a year later, after I completed my training. Instead of being promoted to front office assistant manager, I was offered an assistant housekeeping manager position in New Orleans—far from the role I had worked toward. I was shocked, insulted and devastated. I had been a star trainee and a role model for the others. Would they have offered me the same position if I had been white or a male? I was confused. This was the beginning of feeling the real effects of the "isms"—sexism, racism and ageism. I had to overcome these challenges, hurdles and brick walls—not glass ceilings—as I pursued my career as a hospitality executive.

Despite the solid foundation my parents had given me—a privileged education, exposure to the best opportunities and the ability to navigate different social environments—it still felt like it was never enough. I grew up on the Upper East Side of Manhattan in a diverse apartment building that gave me access to the best resources. I attended Catholic school, got good grades, played sports and learned leadership values and lessons. I attended and graduated from a prestigious all-women's college with a degree in business administration. I couldn't figure out what more I needed to do. I had done everything "they" had told me to do to succeed.

I learned to talk "right" by speaking the Queen's English. I attended Charm School so that I would be socially adept in a variety of environments. I learned what little girls becoming young women should know. I learned to walk right, eat right and speak politely in social circles. I played sports and learned the essence of teamwork. I learned how to win and lose gracefully. I was on the high school student government team and learned to lead at a young age. I was groomed and prepared for success. After all, that is what private prep schools do. I was taught how to cross over and assimilate into different socio, religious, and ethnic circles. I was taught how to survive and thrive.

I was used to being a star. I was the MVP and captain of my team. I worked hard to learn how to pass the social and life tests. I had difficult encounters with teachers from time to time, but I was able to shake them off and keep going. The one test that always took me by surprise was how to succeed when faced with sexism and racism. I was taught that if I worked hard, my race and gender would not matter. This was the lie I had believed for years.

Though I'd had a taste of sexism and racism when I was in high school and college, I had yet to learn how to navigate the challenge of rejection and being denied opportunities clearly because of the color of my skin, my age or my gender. When I began my career, I was determined not to be deterred or derailed. I thought I could stuff the feelings of not being seen or good enough, put on my big-girl panties and keep going.

I soon learned, though, that navigating politics in the work environment was exhausting and stressful. To survive, I just thought I had to work harder. Before I knew it, working became my drug of choice. Pursuing achievement and success drove me in ways I became ashamed of. I had lost my authentic self by trying to be what others told me to be instead of remaining true to who I was. I was just trying to reach my goal.

And as the story goes, addiction affects every part of your life, and this became true for me. Ten years and seven promotions later, I had developed habits and a lifestyle that were unhealthy. I wasn't paying my bills. I wasn't showing up to family events. I was not sleeping well. I was depressed. I was anxious. I gained weight, and I was partying too much. I was burned out and didn't know what to do about any of this. After all, I was in leadership and fearfully suffering in silence. I was too embarrassed to tell anyone what was really happening. I was unable to ask for help. I felt trapped. I found out later that the 10-year plan was based on the experiences of white males and not on the experiences of women, particularly women of color. My mom was right. I was not them.

Thank God for good girlfriends and female mentors. I was having coffee with a girlfriend, and she looked me dead in the face and said, "Elaine, you look like hell." At that point, I realized I had been on a 10-year run to the general manager's position and had not stopped. I was worn out from "doing," worn out and angry from being overlooked. My teammates told me I was hard to work with and really unpleasant to be around. I realized I had become a human "doing" and had given up on living like a human "being." I had bought into the other lie that doing more would get me to my goal.

I realized that I was, indeed, an addict. I was addicted to my work, achievement and success. I realized I had tried to pursue my career goals and dreams alone. I realized that I needed a support team that included female mentors I could identify with. I needed a therapist to help me heal from relational and workplace injuries of injustice. Lastly, I realized I had left my faith at home and never brought it to the workplace. I began reconnecting with God, and my pastors are now part of my life support team.

My self-care and self-actualization journey started in the lobby of Loews New York Hotel over a cup of coffee. I now know that we cannot navigate the challenges of life without community, without mentors, without women who look like us. For the last 20 years, I have been honored to mentor, coach and train women to ascend to senior positions in the C- suite to disrupt embedded systems of injustice.

Looking back, I understand the wisdom in my mother's words. The rules of the game are indeed different for those who don't fit the traditional mold, especially for women of color in leadership in America. While hard work, education and determination are essential, they are not always enough to overcome systemic barriers. I achieved my goal. I became a general manager in 17 years. I attained my goal with a supportive community.

One of the most important lessons I've learned after years in senior leadership positions in the hospitality industry is that it's crucial to recognize and navigate these barriers without losing sight of your authentic self. I realized I had a specific feminine power, a critical voice to exercise. Second, my experience taught me resilience and the importance of advocating for oneself, even in the face of disappointment. Last, I also learned that

YOU ARE NOT THEM

our journeys are different, and they are not to be compared.

Ultimately, success isn't just about following a prescribed formula; it's about understanding your unique obstacles and finding ways to overcome them with grace and tenacity. Each path to success is unique. My mother's words reminded me to stay vigilant, woke, aware of the challenges ahead and most importantly, to stay in a community of people who are candid in love, allowing you to live, love and lead yourself and others with grace. Remember, our pain can lead us to our purpose.

Elaine Robinson Beattie

Elaine Robinson Beattie spends her days passionately working with leaders in the marketplace and ministry as they pursue their purpose. She is a trailblazing leader, speaker and author whose journey from the operations of Fortune 500 companies to the forefront of women's leadership advocacy has inspired countless lives. With over 30 years of executive experience in the hospitality industry, Elaine broke through barriers as one of the few Black women to rise to the top echelons of corporate America. As the CEO of the Women of Vision Leadership Institute, she is dedicated to empowering women—especially women of color—to lead with authenticity, grace, and resilience.

Elaine's expertise in leadership development, combined with her profound understanding of the challenges women face in the workplace, has made her a sought-after mentor and leadership coach. Her signature programs, including the transformative Lead Wise Lead Well Management Training, boast an impressive track record of propelling leaders to the executive ranks.

YOU ARE NOT THEM

A graduate of Simmons College, with advanced degrees in management, leadership and religious leadership, Elaine brings a unique blend of business acumen, spiritual wisdom and social justice advocacy to her work. Through her writings, speeches and coaching, she continues to inspire a new generation of leaders to navigate and transform the systems that often hold them back.

Elaine may be reached at Elaine@Elainespeaking.com or www.elainespeaking.com.

CHASING 100

Dreams Do Come True

By Fredricia Cunegin

17 years old.
In labor, 12 hours.
A beautiful caramel-tone baby girl, 7 lbs., 7 oz.
Then, I looked up, and my daddy was smiling, but he shouldn't have been smiling.

It was a beautiful sunny day, the kind where the sky is a perfect shade of blue, and the warmth on your skin fills you with a sense of boundless possibility. I remember it like it was yesterday. The bus finally came to a halt with a gentle hiss, and as I stepped off, it felt like I was crossing a threshold into a new world. My heart raced with the excitement of the unknown. This was the day I officially became a high school student—a milestone that put me just three years away from my lifelong dream of becoming a college graduate. But I don't want to get ahead of myself; instead, I invite you to walk with me along this adventurous path.

The year was 1975. I was a music major at the prestigious McKinley Tech High School, perched majestically on a sprawling hill in the Northeast corridor of Washington, D.C. The school stood like a beacon of opportunity, its hallways buzzing with life. As students hurried from class to class, the air was filled with the sounds of laughter, the clacking of slamming lockers, and the rhythmic shuffle of feet on polished floors. It was a world teeming with energy and possibilities, and I quickly found myself adapting to the new rhythm and systematic expectations that came with being a high school student.

As a music major, I had Mrs. Guilt's classical chorus classroom as my home base. This was no ordinary room; it was a sanctuary where voices intertwined in harmony, where each day began at 8 a.m. sharp with the rich, resonant tones of trained vocals echoing through the corridors. This classroom was more than just a place to learn music; it was a space where dreams took root. Conversations about college campuses sparked something deep within me. Some of my classmates confidently spoke about following in their parents' footsteps, attending alma maters that had shaped generations before them. It was fascinating and a little intimidating. While I knew I wanted a college degree, the specifics—where I would go and how I would pay for it—were still shrouded in uncertainty. Yet, in my heart, one thing was clear: I was college-bound.

My journey was also deeply rooted in the legacy of my family. I come from a lineage of pastors—a legacy of faith and service. My paternal grandmother was a pastor, and she built a church that stands strong to this day. My parents, too, were pastors, dedicating 45 years of their lives to loving God and humanity and serving others with unwavering devotion. They were the embodiment of first-class servant leaders, and from them, my siblings and I learned the values of hard work, love for God and commitment to serving others. These teachings became the bedrock of my life, the foundational truth that guides me even today.

When I got home after that first day of high school, I was giddy with excitement. I eagerly shared every detail with my parents. They listened intently, hanging onto every word, their faces reflecting the pride and hope they felt for my future. I was excited, too—not just for what high school would bring but for the endless possibilities ahead.

One of the first lessons I learned as a high school student was that upper-level and first-year students may for various reasons be enrolled in the same classes. This is how I met John Smith*, a senior football player who had decided to graduate early. He was cute, funny, well-known and had a great personality. He met me at my locker, walked me to my classes and walked me to the bus stop at the end of each day. His dream was to graduate a year early, and of course, I was still focused on becoming a college graduate.

High school students could leave campus during their lunch break, and one day, John invited me to have lunch with him in his car. I was hesitant; I had never been invited to a guy's car, but I thought it was okay since his vehicle was parked in the school parking lot. Just before it was time to return to class, John lit a joint and invited me to participate, and I smoked a joint for the first time. I felt weird and wanted sweets. I told myself I was not doing that again.

By the end of the first semester, my grades were decent, but sadly, I had indulged in smoking marijuana, missing classes, and working hard to stay upbeat. My friends noticed a change in my behavior and enthusiasm. While I was present and on time for my 8 a.m. music choral class, I was not spending as much time with my best friends at lunch, at games or at special events because I was spending more time with John, who had decided not to graduate early.

A new year began. I was a sophomore and decided to get back on track and stay focused because I was only two years away from becoming a college student. I shared my decision to stay focused with John; he was unhappy with my decision, but I was determined to keep on track. I had excellent teachers, especially the women; they recognized the threads of the web that entangled me. One day, after class, my history instructor told me I had so much to offer and that I needed to love myself and stay focused. Little did I know just how prevalent her voice would become.

Mid-semester, I began to feel sick and tired, unsure why, but I maintained my daily routine. I was late—not for class or submitting an assignment; my monthly menstrual cycle was late. Oh, my God! I was devastated!! I had tell my parents that their 16-year-old baby girl was pregnant. My parents grieved. My daddy was so disappointed that for a brief time (which felt like an eternity) he didn't talk to me. I often wondered if my daddy would smile again. I felt so humiliated when the congregation learned that I was pregnant. Imagine church members who would immediately stop talking when I walked by, making me feel like I was the topic of discussion. Being at church became unbearable; my parents allowed me to stay home on Sundays. My life was shattered, but I can honestly say that I experienced the essence of servant leadership through my parents during those dark days.

On July 27, 1977, I gave birth to my beautiful, healthy baby girl, who weighed 7 pounds and 7 ounces. I graduated from high school on June 5, 1978, and enrolled at the University of Maryland College Park. My daddy smiled.

I was 18 years old, a teenage mom, a high school graduate and a college student, and I was on public assistance. My monthly check allowed me to purchase what I needed for my beautiful baby girl and to save a little money. My mother was my built-in babysitter, the best! I attended classes during the day, and when I got home, my mother ensured that my daughter was ready to spend time with me. This system was working, but the worst part of this process was the intense disrespect I routinely experienced when I had to engage with employees of the public assistance program. It got so bad that I decided to withdraw from school, and in 1981, I became an employee. I walked away from what appeared to be my lifelong dream of graduating from college. This was one of the saddest days of my life.

As I progressed, I enrolled at the University of Maryland University College (UMUC), now the University of Maryland Global Campus (UMGC). I took night classes, and occasionally, I would take my daughter with me. However, I ran out of money, so the dream was on hold. In 1986, I married the love of my life, Irvin Cunegin. We became a blended family with two daughters. My husband, a speech pathologist, was passionate about education; he began talking to me about completing my dream of becoming a college graduate. I chuckled and said, "It

is too late." He continued to encourage me until I said yes! And this is what happened:
- At 37, I graduated from the University of Maryland University College with a bachelor's degree in psychology, but I did not stop there:
- At 45, I started HR In-Motion LLC, a human resource management consultancy, but I did not stop there:
- At 52, I graduated from the University of Maryland University College with a master's degree in management and a concentration in human resource management.
- I have built my HR consultancy into a six-figure organization, with more to come.
- My daddy's smile was back!

Dreams do come true!

Fredricia Cunegin

Fredricia Cunegin, the president/CEO of HRinMotion LLC (HRIM), brings more than 20 years of experience working with for-profit and non-profit organizations as a certified DISC (dominance, influence, steadiness, and conscientious practitioner) supporting organizations in building strong teams with effective skillsets. She serves as an executive coach in two communities with a passionate focus on building legacy leaders who offer HRIM a continual platform to provide leadership-style training services that produce (1) congruency with organizations, (2) caliber expertise and value presented to organizations, and (3) continuity that exists through succession planning.

Fredricia has successfully provided training services to the District of Columbia Department of Human Resource Center for Learning and Development and DC HR and has taught courses such as but not limited to Building a Professional Vision, Train-the-Trainer and The Power of Effective Communication. She has presented leadership training such as Your Vision and Performance Produces Excellent Quality to leaders of the Food Safety and Inspection

DREAMS DO COME TRUE

Services (FSIS) United States Department of Agriculture (USDA) and has presented sexual harassment training to team members of the National Industries for the Blind (NIB).

Fredricia has earned the professional human resource (PHR) certification conferred by the Human Resource Certification Institute (HRCI) and the SHRM-CP certification conferred by the Society of Human Resource Management (SHRM). She also holds a Master of Science Management (MSM) degree with a human resource management concentration from the University of Maryland University Global Campus.

She may be reached at fcunegin@hrinmotionllc.com.

CHASING 100

Live and Lead Your Life Unleashed

By Gary Hibbs

"I want to live."

My therapist had just asked, "What are you doing here?" From the outside, I had it all. An incredible wife. Four beautiful children. Great career. Big house. Church leader.

But I was dying.

I played it safe and was in hiding. I wouldn't let you know me, afraid to risk being really known because if you knew the real me, you might reject me. And I couldn't face that. I was alone. I was isolated. I was disconnected. I would sense what would make you happy and adjust to that.

I lived over half a century making sure that I didn't mess anything up in your eyes. I wanted to make sure I was a good guy—or, at least, that you thought I was. People around me essentially controlled me. Life was about external conformance. I always seemed like a "nice" guy because I would ask you a lot of questions, and it looked like I was interested in you. But I was just protecting myself from you getting to know me.

My goal in life was to selfishly build my reputation. But a reputation is only who people think you are. Character is who you really are. I lacked character because I didn't know who I really was. I let you define "me."

I was an actor. In fact, the word "hypocrite" comes from the Greek word, "hypokrites," which means "an actor." I was a hypocrite. And it didn't feel good at all. I lived multiple acts, depending on who I was around.

Acting was exhausting, and I was tired.
You're only as sick as the secrets you keep. I was getting sicker all the time.

I once asked my high school sweetheart this question out of nowhere: "What do you think about the inner me?"

She must've thought, "What's his problem?" The scary thing was this: I didn't even know what I was asking. I just knew that there was someone inside of me trying to get out and be free.

If you are never really known, you never know if you are genuinely loved. I didn't even know who I was. How, therefore, could I be loved? I was increasingly in despair and alone, inside of myself.

I knew something was missing. I missed a sense of connection, a sense of belonging, a sense of community, of peace. I missed having an integrated life, and I didn't have a sense of home.

You remember the Scrooge character in the Dickens novel? When accompanied by one of the ghosts, he is amongst a group of people supposed to be family, but they can't see him. He sees them, but it's as if he isn't even there. I increasingly identified with that character. No one saw me. I was there physically, but increasingly, my feelings and real thoughts were invisible, trapped inside. I didn't belong or feel safe.

Author and philosopher Henry David Thoreau said, "The mass of men live lives of quiet desperation." That was me. The lonely tears inside became showers of rain. I wouldn't let people in, and I wouldn't come out of the rain and my self-imposed prison. I remember playing hide-and-seek as a kid and hiding so well that no one would find me. I became so lonesome after a while that I soon hoped that someone would find me, but I was afraid to let them. Awful!

LIVE AND LEAD YOUR LIFE UNLEASHED

What would deliver me?
Who or what would find me?

With this growing desperation and a sense of not having any connection or control over my life, I would collect and control things—baseball cards when I was a child, books when I became an adult. I could hoard and control these things, and I became increasingly isolated from people. My best friends were on cardboard and paper—not real, live human beings.

Isolation is one of the most frightening things to human beings. Even the "tough guys" in prison hate to be thrown into isolation, or "solitary." We are created for community and connection!

But for me, the fear of being found out as an imposter was still greater than the pain of isolation. I was in a terrible double bind, lonely and afraid.

I especially feared intimacy, the ultimate exposure! I couldn't let anyone, especially my wife, know me. The thought of her rejecting me was my worst fear. I left my wife and kids knocking on the door of my heart, but I couldn't answer. The darkness, pain and shame grew worse. I needed a pain reliever.

I didn't drink alcohol until I was in graduate school. (It would have hurt my reputation!) The first time I drank alcohol, I felt instant peace. It felt wonderful to escape. I didn't drink often, but when I did, there was a good chance I'd "blackout":. I'd still function but lose memory of what had occurred. These instances were infrequent, but they served as a dangerous and ultimately destructive escape valve. And the hiding worsened. There was no way anyone could know about this!

Relational isolation and lockdown became worse, as did the guilt and shame of secret drinking and its related behavior. It was hell. I increasingly distanced myself from everyone, and 24 years into my marriage, I had a DUI. I was horrified to think that someone would find out.

I needed help but didn't seek it; I was too proud. I needed to protect my reputation, of course! I couldn't see that I lacked integrity or that I was living in dis-integrity. I was disintegrating and crumbling, just like a building that lacks integrity.

Einstein says that the definition of insanity is doing the same thing repeatedly and expecting different results. I kept doing the same things hoping for different results, but the results stayed the same. It was insane.

After another DUI, I went to jail. Lying on a cold, concrete floor and dressed in an orange jumpsuit, I surrendered. I was desperate. I couldn't do it anymore! It was a severe mercy and gift of God, this gift of desperation. I said to God, "Whatever it takes, I need to get help."

What I heard from God was what I'd heard most all my life: "I love you. Period. Just as you really are. No need to perform for anyone. I will never abandon or reject you." For the first time, I trusted with both my head and heart that this was true. I surrendered.

I finally let go and was unleashed from the ultimate fear of rejection. In that moment, I felt an incredible rush of peace. It was the beginning of healing and freedom.

Nonetheless, there were consequences.

I came home from rehab to separation papers. I learned that you can push people away for only so long. Eventually, they'll tire of you keeping your distance, and they will simply walk away. My family grew weary of knocking on the door to my heart. It never opened as I hid. They left. They never really knew me because I wouldn't let them. As I was waking up, they headed for the exit doors.

Eventually, I lost a lot—my marriage, the affection of my kids, my career.

I tried to argue for grace and mercy. But you can't talk your way out of something that you've acted your way into.

When hiding and in pain, we medicate and distract, thinking those things will bring relief. They don't. All addictions make promises but don't deliver. They distract us from being whole and real and present and free. We stay busy; we turn to sports, shopping, food, gambling, sex, Netflix, alcohol—anything to distract and ease the pain.

LIVE AND LEAD YOUR LIFE UNLEASHED

Thankfully, I hit a point where I said, "Enough!" My painful discontent had crystallized.

This was the "gift of desperation" I needed. I surrendered to live 100. All in, not half-hearted and hiding. Half-hearted living is not living at all. It's boring and dull. To really live, we need to be all in and live all-out, free from false identities: Unleashed!

How? It's a simple acronym, H-O-W. "H"…be honest. "O"…be open. "W"….be willing. It's simple in concept and profound in impact. It works! It's never too late. It takes acceptance. And grace. And courage. And action.

I stopped play-acting and became vulnerable and real, knowing God's love is unconditional. Today, I'm not falling apart. I'm coming together. I'm not dis-integrating. I'm integrated. I'm not half-hearted. I am whole-hearted. I'm not incongruent. I'm congruent!

In fact, on the one-year date of my sobriety, I was literally standing on top of Mt. Kilimanjaro. So cool. Life.

If you're locked in your head, hiding, all alone and isolated in there, trying to fight that crazy committee of voices that tells you you're not enough, you don't have to stay there. You can get out. You can write new chapters, a new story. The pen is in your hand… keep writing with freedom!

You can choose to be free and climb from a dark valley to a mountaintop. Leave it all on the field. Chase 100. Be unleashed.

That's where life is!

Gary Hibbs

Gary Hibbs is the CEO and founder of Unleashed to Lead LLC, a company whose mission is to help leaders lead themselves well in order to lead others well.

After years as a high-level executive, Gary saw his life crash, as he was hiding in the pursuit of perfecting an image and reputation rather than developing an integrated character from the inside out.

Recognizing that hidden despair and emptiness can be caused by fear, bad habits, unfulfilling work settings and misplaced values, Gary is convinced that many leaders are isolated and hiding in their fears, desperate to be free to lead themselves well. His passion is to help leaders in hiding find freedom. As he says, "We need to be unleashed to lead!"

With Juris Doctor and Master of Social Work degrees, Hibbs is a seasoned leader with over 35 years of experience in the senior living field. He is the CEO and president of Knollwood in northwest Washington, D.C. He is a certified coach, speaker and trainer with the John Maxwell Leadership Team and utilizes the Maxwell DISC as a trainer and consultant. He speaks to groups

LIVE AND LEAD YOUR LIFE UNLEASHED

large and small and id s coach to teams and individuals. After serving as an attorney with the Prince George's County Senior Law Project, Gary invested 27 years with Erickson Senior Living in various roles, including serving as the executive director of Riderwood Village, the nation's largest continuing care retirement community in Silver Spring, Md. He has served on the board of Adventist's White Oak Medical Center and is a trustee with the Healthcare Council and ShareSource. Gary is also an adjunct professor at the UMBC Erickson School of Aging, shaping the education of future professionals in the field. He was married for 31 years and is the father of four adult children and two grandchildren.

You may reach Gary at
www.unleashedtolead.com
gary@unleashedtolead.com
410-303-5088

CHASING 100

The Dreamer's Heart

By Dr. Hermione Jourdan

Life has a way of shaping us through its disappointments and challenges. I remember those early days filled with wonder, believing wholeheartedly that I could be anything I wanted. The world felt like a vast playground, full of dreams and adventures waiting to be discovered. My heart was hopeful and my spirit untouched by life's harsh realities. I saw endless possibilities and believed I was destined for greatness.

But as the years went by, something shifted. For some, this shift is subtle and distant, while for others, it marks a vivid moment—the day innocence is lost. For me, it was the unexpected loss of my husband. That loss shook me to my core, turning my world upside down. My once-clear and vibrant vision of the future became clouded with sorrow and confusion. For the first time, I truly understood the weight of pain and felt profound hopelessness. The world no longer made sense, and I found myself living between two worlds—one filled with daily responsibilities and one that now felt like a distant dream.

Each visit to that dream left me more broken and lost. I remember standing in my living room, feeling an overwhelming emptiness, like I was truly losing myself. In that vulnerable moment, I softly whispered, "It is well with my soul," trying to convince myself of a peace that seemed so distant.

I no longer recognized the person I once was. It felt like I had lost a vital part of myself, leaving me adrift and uncertain about who I had become or where I belonged. The hardest part was realizing that I didn't like who I had become. It seemed all the joy had drained from my life, leaving behind bitterness and an inability to truly feel anything. I had become a shell of the vibrant person I once was. Deep down, I knew this wasn't who I wanted to be.

In response to the pain, I began to construct my life around moments of despair. I erected emotional altars at those places of hurt, returning to them whenever I faced new disappointments. I told myself, "I knew it all along; it was just a matter of time before someone let me down." Fear and anxiety became my constant companions, shaping my views and becoming the lenses through which I navigated life. My experiences began to overshadow the hopeful innocence of my youth and shaped the person I was becoming.

The routine of life and my circumstances began to dim my inner light. Without even realizing it, I shifted from living and dreaming to merely surviving. The joy and curiosity that once defined me became distant memories. Life became a series of tasks and obligations. The Pursuit of Success

As I realized the world wasn't what I thought, I grappled with a deep sense of disillusionment. What was I to do with this newfound knowledge? As a young woman, I tried to stay in control, meticulously planning my future. I thought, "What if I could find joy in a career, a title that would bring not only prestige but also money, comfort, freedom and most of all, security?" I chased the next big thing, believing the next promotion, achievement or accolade would bring fulfillment.

I raced from one goal to the next, with little time for reflection or gratitude. The demands of my career and societal pressures consumed my energy. Despite appearing successful, I felt disconnected from my true self, as if living someone else's dream. The relentless pace left me longing for deeper connections and a sense of purpose beyond material gain. The things I thought would bring happiness often left me feeling empty.

When my career no longer fed my soul, I sought joy in the pursuit of success and achievement. I accumulated possessions and accolades—homes, cars, careers that once promised fulfillment but now felt hollow. The thrill of new experiences faded quickly, leaving me perpetually unsatisfied. I began to wonder if there was more to life.

The Valley of Grief

Grief is a deeply personal journey, and we all experience it differently. But I want to share what I've learned and how I've walked through my own valleys, clinging to hope that comes from above.

When tragedy struck, I found myself at the altar of despair again, questioning every dream and desire. Why hope? Why want anything when it can be snatched away in an instant? It's all so fleeting, like Solomon said: chasing after the wind, sand slipping through my fingers. In the depths of despair, I wondered if I'd ever feel normal again. When would the sun's warmth touch my skin? When would the pain cease? Grief cast its shadows so dark that the sun seemed hidden forever. Food lost its flavor; laughter became hollow, and every breath felt like a struggle. It was like being lost at sea, waves relentlessly crashing against me. I dove so deep, thinking I might never resurface. Sometimes, I even wished not to. I once heard of a woman who wanted to swim around the world but stopped just short of the shore, thinking she had miles to go, only to realize she was almost there. In my darkest moments, I often can't see how close I am to the shore.

But even in my deepest despair, I found reasons to come back up for air. I discovered three precious reasons to keep fighting—my girls. So, when I resurfaced, I looked up. I admit that I felt angry, as if God had failed me. Why give something only to take it away? What's the point of it all? But here's what I hold on to: even when I don't understand the why, I trust in God's plan, a plan to prosper me, not to harm me, a plan to give me hope and a future. I still have a million questions and no answers, but faith is trusting even when I can't see the full picture.

The Masks We Wear

Even moments of joy were tinged with anxiety, as I feared their fleeting nature. I wore masks of contentment, hiding my turmoil as I strived for more wealth and success. The pursuit of happiness became a burden, draining me of time and energy that could be spent on meaningful relationships and personal growth. I was left wondering if true fulfillment would ever be within my grasp. I started to question the choices I had made and the paths I had taken.

I struggled to balance the demands of work and family, haunted by guilt over missed opportunities to cherish the moments that truly mattered. The pursuit of success and recognition seemed hollow in the face of my deepest regrets and unfulfilled desires. I began to see that the things I had placed so much importance on were not what truly mattered. Despite my best efforts, I was discontented and weary, yearning for relief from the pressures of life. I realized too late the toll my choices had taken on my health, relationships and spiritual well-being. I was left questioning the meaning of it all, wondering if there was a path to peace and fulfillment amidst the chaos. I longed for something deeper, something that would bring true peace to my soul.

The Path to Redemption

Amidst my struggles, I observed those who had discovered a deeper truth. They found joy in simplicity and gratitude, showing resilience and steadfastness in the face of adversity. Their faith in God's plan gave them peace and purpose, even when life's storms threatened to overwhelm them. They reminded me that true fulfillment comes not from what we acquire but from who we become in the process. Their lives were a testament to the power of faith and the strength that comes from knowing God's plan.

Amidst life's trials, I saw those who seemed to defy despair. Despite profound loss and scarcity, they exuded a spirit of resilience and gratitude. They found solace in serving others—tending to the sick, comforting the widow and uplifting the downtrodden. Their ability to find purpose in hardship stood in stark contrast to my own struggle to fill an inner void. They taught me that there is a greater purpose in life than just seeking my own happiness.

A Journey of Becoming

I learned that finding joy was not about accolades, possessions, or titles. It was about the journey of becoming who I was meant to be, finding peace in my faith, and living a life of purpose and meaning. In the midst of my pain, something shifted. I realized that life, with all its uncertainties and heartaches, was something I had to confront head-on. And in this confrontation, I discovered that I wasn't alone. I found strength I didn't know I had—a resilience that came from seeking help from above.

I now rest in the assurance that my heavenly Father cares for me. He provides for my needs and offers me peace. By aligning my life with his purpose, I experience true joy and fulfillment, regardless of my circumstances. As I cultivate a heart of gratitude and service, I become a channel of his love and grace to those around me, bringing light to a world desperately in need of hope. So, I hold on to those reasons to live. I look up, seek my help from above and believe that even in the darkest valleys, there is a plan for hope and a future. I'm not alone in this journey, and the sun will shine on me again. Though the pain is real, and the journey is tough, I keep fighting; I keep looking up, and I trust that even in the darkest valleys, there's a purpose and a plan. I'm not alone in this journey, and neither are you.

Dr. Hermione Jourdan

Dr. Hermione Jourdan is a mother of three and a dedicated professional whose life has been shaped by a deep commitment to helping others. Her journey began with a bachelor's degree from Florida Atlantic University. Driven by a passion for holistic healthcare, she pursued her education at Palmer College of Chiropractic, where she discovered her true calling. As a board-certified chiropractic physician, Dr. Hermione focuses on treating the root causes of pain and discomfort, offering her patients a path to healthier, happier lives.

With over a decade of experience in healthcare coordination, Dr. Hermione transitioned into the home care industry, founding Tree of Life Premier Services. Her company was born out of a belief that everyone deserves exceptional care, especially within the comfort of their own homes. Through Tree of Life, Dr. Hermione provides compassionate, dignified care to the elderly, offering peace of mind to families and inspiring others through her dedicated service.

Dr. Hermione's commitment extends beyond her professional

THE DREAMER'S HEART

life. Her faith is central to her values, and she is actively involved in her local church, where she serves and supports various missions. One mission particularly close to her heart is Mercy Ships, an organization that delivers life-transforming medical care to those in need around the world.

Pursuing one's passion is one of life's greatest joys, and Dr. Hermione is blessed to live out that passion every day—whether through her chiropractic practice, her work with Tree of Life, or her community service. Her ultimate goal is to serve, inspire, and make a lasting impact on the lives of those she touches, while steadfastly upholding the mission and core values that guide her in everything she does.

Dr. Hermione may be reached at Drjourdan03@gmail.com.

CHASING 100

Living Beyond the Labels

By James Keith Powers

I spent most of my life living behind the bars of an invisible cage, feeling trapped by the labels people placed on me. These labels shaped how people saw me, and more dangerously, how I began to see myself. But deep down, in the quiet corners of my soul, I knew I was more than what others labeled me to be. I felt a fire, a restless energy, an unspoken potential waiting to be unleashed. Yet, no one ever told me I could be better. No one ever said, "You have more to give." But I knew. And that knowledge, that unyielding belief in the possibility of something greater, became the fuel for my journey.

My mom was a young single mother of five kids, and she knew how to survive. She was the master of stretching—stretching a dollar, a meal and even an argument when she was upset. When she and my father divorced, she went into survival mode. Being the oldest, I became her sidekick, the Robin to her Batman. She taught me that to survive, you have to be a great manager under pressure. I watched her manage the house with little to no resources. Although she was under a lot of pressure and felt inadequate at times, she never allowed her emotions to affect her ability to keep moving forward. She taught me to be resilient, to trust that no matter how bad things seemed, we could withstand them.

One winter my mom had to choose between buying us a few toys for Christmas or paying the light bill. She decided to buy us clothes. I said that she would figure out the light bill later. That

CHASING 100

Christmas was one of the best we'd ever had, but it all came to an end when the lights suddenly shut off in 40-degree weather. My mom was panicking because she had no money, no car and nowhere else for us to stay. To make matters worse, we had guests over when the lights went out. As our guests were gathering their things in the dark to leave, I heard someone giggling and saying that my mom was broke. This didn't affect mom in the slightest; she put on her coat, went outside and caught up to the electric company employee. She told him she was a single parent of five children and asked him not to leave us in the cold. The man looked at my mom, opened the electric box and turned the power back on, saying, "God bless you." We never experienced anything like that again, but I learned that my mom never lived in a prison of other people's opinions. She always made decisions that were in her best interest.

Being one of the poor kids in school left me insecure and depressed. My clothes, my shoes—everything about me—was ridiculed. I hated school. I skipped classes as often as I could, missing the maximum number of days allowed just to avoid the torment. When I did attend, I would escape into daydreams about the life I wanted, places I wanted to go, things I wanted to be. But then the bell would ring, snapping me back to reality. I failed the ninth grade because of missing too many days of school. My teacher told me I was a failure and that I would never amount to anything. I wouldn't have thought a teacher would say something like that. What she didn't realize was I spent most of my time blocking out the noise of the kids laughing at the clothes I wore. I literally had two pairs of pants to wear. My brother and I were close in size, and we swapped out pants every couple of days. I felt so disconnected and out of place. How could my teacher not see the pain in my eyes? How could she, as a teacher, not see my greatness? If my teacher couldn't recognize my greatness, then maybe there was nothing great to notice. I was at one of my lowest points, left wondering how one could chase a dream when the dream seemed impossible, how one could chase a dream when nothing suggested the dream could happen, how one could chase a dream when the dreamer had already been labeled a failure. I graduated from high school without a clue about what my next steps would be. I was afraid of college because I was labeled too stupid to go; I considered working at the local factory, but I was already labeled too lazy, and because I lived in a bad neighborhood, I was labeled a criminal. The labels made me feel I was ill-equipped, and I was too afraid to try anything.

Despite my fear, I took a chance and joined the Army. That's when my life changed. The Army showed me the possibilities of becoming more than others thought of me. I realized the reason I was having so many issues was because I was in the wrong environment.

I learned when I was young and farmed watermelons with my granddad that not all plants grow in every environment. Some conditions are too harsh for some plants to grow and bear fruit. You might have to move the plant to a place where it can flourish. I learned that this applies to people, too.

When I moved away, I realized that I had struggled because of the limited beliefs inherent in my environment. I had adopted those limiting beliefs because that's all I knew. But when my environment changed, I began to do things I never thought possible. I learned that it's okay to try new things, to take risks, to stop playing it safe. The world was bigger than where I came from. Sometimes what limits you is not your inability to grow; it's your inability to grow in certain conditions.

Not only did I begin to grow, I also learned to excel. While stationed in Germany, I had to drive a patrol van to Wiesbaden to pick up an American soldier. The van was a big, square, green vehicle that reminded me of the Scooby-Doo Mystery Machine. This thing was loud and painfully slow, especially on the Autobahn highway where there were stretches with no speed limits. Cars flew by me at close to 200 mph while I was stuck at 50 mph. It was terrifying, and I wondered why the van was so slow. I found out that the van had a governor installed—a device that limited its speed. Without the governor, the van could have gone much faster, operating at the speed it was designed for. That taught me something profound: some people go through life with a governor placed on them, never moving at their maximum speed. When you remove that governor—those limiting beliefs and labels— you realize you are capable of so much more. You are limitless.

The only limits are the ones you put on yourself. My transformation began when I stopped letting others define me. Just because you fail doesn't mean you're a failure. I learned that failure is part of the process, a steppingstone to success. The labels others placed on me were never who I truly was—they were just the limits others imposed on me.

It was in the Army that I started to peel off the labels that had been slapped on me. I thought about all those times I daydreamed in class about places I wanted to go and things I wanted to achieve. The Army took me to those places. I traveled the world, earned two bachelor's degrees and became a best-selling author. I retired as a senior leader and started a leadership program. I realized I was capable of so much more than what the labels people had placed on me said I could (or couldn't) do. I became who God made me to be.

You are more than what people call you. When people label you as something you're not, stop answering to those labels. Remove the governor from your life. Push beyond the limits that others have set for you and that you've set for yourself. Embrace the truth that you are capable of more—you are limitless. Chase 100, because you were designed for so much more than just surviving. You were made to thrive.

LIVING BEYOND THE LABELS

James Keith Powers

James Keith Powers is a licensed ordained minister who holds a bachelor's degree in theology from the Minnesota Graduate School of Theology and a bachelor's degree in behavior science from Ashford University.

James's passion is for mentoring youth/young adults. He serves on the Youth Leader Team at New Life Fellowship Church and leads the mentorship program, Boys to Men, which mentors youth in the Lawton/Ft. Sill, Okla., community.

He is the proud husband of Janette Powers, and they have been married for 13 years. Together they have six children. He served as a soldier in the U.S. Army and retired after 20 years of service. He also is a recipient of the Bronze Star Medal for heroic or meritorious achievement. He is an advocate for Gold Star Families, families who lost their soldiers while the soldier was serving in combat.

James is also the Amazon best-selling author of the book, "Flying Too Low How to Elevate to Your Full Potential."

James Keith has dedicated his life to winning souls for Christ and has the heart of a true servant. Whether it is being in the trenches with the troubled youth in the community or praising God as the praise team leader, he does everything to glorify and reverence God.

James Powers 229-338-2773 - ga_xpress@hotmail.com

RIDE IT LIKE YOU STOLE IT!

By Judy-Ann Davis Young

It never dawned on me to ask anyone's opinion about my passion for motorcycle riding. Yet, those in my social circles were generous with their critiques of my lifestyle, openly shaking their heads at the courage and audacity I had to start riding a motorcycle when I was 50 years old. There were times I knew I was the topic of discussion when I left the room. The snide remarks and fake smiles weren't lost on me. They just weren't important. I'm unapologetic about the intrinsic characteristics of my personality that thirst for adventure and speed. Motorcycling appeases my desire for freedom; the experience is unparalleled.

Being different was not new to me, nor was it intimidating. I grew up in Alaska and spent 23 years working in a non-traditional capacity on the Trans-Alaska Pipeline. This organically granted me a license to bend gender roles to suit my personality. By the time I was 50 years old, I was determined that menopause was not going to rob me of my femininity, vitality, curiosity or—most of all—my passion for living a BIG (Bold, Interesting and Gorgeous) life.

I was unbothered when I heard that women in my social circles were beginning to question my sanity, sexuality and motivation for stepping out of my self-assigned roles of wife, grandmother and insurance agent. It didn't matter to me that they laughed behind my back. I had already learned that life is not a spectator sport; people who judge the most achieve the least.

CHASING 100

Note to Myself: Father Time remains undefeated. No one gets out alive, so enjoy riding the clock out on your own terms.

I was living in Las Vegas, Nevada when I bought my first motorcycle. My "boujee," retired, educated, married friends had migrated to Las Vegas from all over the USA. I moved there seeking adventure, which made me an anomaly; I was neither a city girl nor a country girl. I was just different; growing up listening to dog teams howling at night and watching moose graze in our yard gave me a unique perspective on adventure, and I craved adventure.

I found that riding a motorcycle quenched my thirst for adventure. Merging into freeway traffic, feeling the breeze against my cheeks and the sun on my face, hearing the roar of my exhaust pipes and feeling the vibration of the motor as I shift gears—these combine to give me a rush only a biker understands. By the time I hit cruising speed, I'm in total bliss. Sweet Baby Jesus! This is freedom. With Luther Vandross blaring through the speakers, I smile to myself. Clearly, I'm winning the game of life on my own terms.

Buying that first motorcycle fulfilled a 15-year dream. It was confirmation that dreams don't have expiration dates. When a dream doesn't come to fruition, it's usually because the committee in your head is talking you out of greatness, causing your dreams to fade into obscurity. Note to myself: Pay attention; the mind is a great servant but a terrible master.

For the first time in my life, I was passionate about something that ignited all my senses. Riding requires physical strength, mental focus, quick reflexes and the ability to multitask.

It's also a metaphor for life. Learning to pivot with precision while maintaining balance and momentum is paramount to being successful in life. Riding has taught me how to shift gears, regardless of how steep the climb or how sharp the curves are. This shifting of gears and switching lanes challenged me to step into leadership.

RIDE IT LIKE YOU STOLE IT!

Here is how it happened:

It was late when we checked into the motel in Childress, Texas. I was exhausted and hungry, and I was questioning my decision to sign up for this daunting 25-day, 27-state breast cancer fundraising motorcycle tour. This was the fourth day and fourth state of the tour; we had ridden nonstop through a tumultuous storm between Albuquerque, N.M, and Childress when the tour organizer issued an ultimatum: either follow her rules or leave the ride immediately. As an experienced rider, I knew her proposed rules were unrealistic and grueling. I decided I was done. I would leave the group and finish the ride on my own.

I awakened the chase vehicle driver. I needed to get my gear out of the truck. He grumbled under his breath, saying, "Why can't y'all get along?", but his words fell on deaf ears.

Mentally, I was shifting gears and planning the rest of my trip. I pulled my gear to the rear of the truck, and when I turned around, three of my fellow riders—Kim, Tammy and Gayle—were standing behind me. They said, "We are leaving with you. We respect and trust you more than we do the organizer."

Stunned and humbled by this, I nodded, "Okay!" I had a flashback to my life coach, Jane, who had told me: "JudyAnn, be prepared to step into leadership; things may not go as planned." I had prepared all my life for this moment.

By 6 a.m. we heard the chase vehicle and three motorcycles pulling out of the motel. We were 1,500 miles from home and were fending for ourselves. I took a deep breath. I was the only rider with cross-country experience. I had the women call their families to tell them things had changed, that I was the new road captain and that I promised to get them safely back to California. I knew the women needed a morale booster.

Our first stop was Dallas, where we ate authentic Mexican food and sipped margaritas. The women began to feel hopeful. Riding into Louisiana, I felt an exhilarating sense of freedom. Any doubt I had when I left Childress had dissipated. Our guardian angels were watching over us, and as I allowed God to order my steps, I knew we would be fine. Note to Myself: Fear and faith cannot occupy the same space; courageous women move with an air of confidence and conviction.

We mastered a smooth riding formation, and by the time we got to New Orleans, we were confident and competent as we moved easily through traffic. We saw remnants of the devastation of Hurricane Katrina, yet it didn't diminish the mystique of "N'awlins," a city known for its food, music and rich history. As the sun was setting on New Orleans, we headed across the Pontchartrain Bridge toward Biloxi, Miss.

At our last gas stop for the night, one of our riders had a medical episode. A combination of the heat and missed medications disoriented her. Working together as a team we got our fallen rider into a hotel bed and her bike to the hotel. By morning our sister rider was feeling ready to continue our tour. Note to Myself: Expect the unexpected; don't panic; always trust your instincts.

By the time we reached the New Jersey turnpike, Kim, Tammy and Gayle were taking turns leading the group. I marveled as these women, who had never ridden outside California, displayed a level of personal fortitude that enhanced their inner beauty and oozed confidence into every facet of their lives. They were walking, talking and moving differently. I'm not saying we were bad-ass; I'm saying we were breathing rare motorcycle air: In 2006, less than 10% of bikers were women, and even fewer women were cross-country riders.

Note to Myself: An empowered woman stands on business; she doesn't cower down when facing a challenge.

Thanks to our friends Linden Bob, Gator, Kas and Holly, our stay in New Jersey was delightful. They provided us with housing and a vehicle to drive while our bikes were being serviced. Our tour was full of opportunities to let go and let God work his magic.

We didn't allow hiccups to derail or stop us from enjoying our experience. From Childress, Texas, to Fort Pierce, Fla.; from Ground Zero in New York City to San Francisco, Calif; we earned what bikers call "street cred," (credibility). We rode over 8,531 miles on our tour for a worthy cause. The money we raised was donated to MD Anderson Breast Cancer Research Center.

At our last gas stop, we lingered to hug and bid each other goodbye. There was nothing left unsaid between us. We had all faced our personal challenges and opportunities to grow. We sat a little taller as we started our bikes for the last leg of our epic journey. As we merged into freeway traffic, I smiled as the familiar breeze caressed my suntanned cheeks. Each woman peeled off at her exit. I watched the San Francisco skyline come into focus as tears of gratitude mingled with the dirt on my suntanned face. Wow. I fulfilled my promise. I got them safely back to California. Too exhausted to ride home, I stored my bike at my friend Mary's house for a week. I felt accomplished, acknowledged and awestruck on the flight home. I had really done it! A week later, I returned to California to ride my bike back to Las Vegas… solo.

I learned how menopause, traditional roles and naysayers have something in common: They can easily rob you of your dreams, sassiness and courage. Your talent, passions and dreams are personal gifts. It's a travesty of justice if you allow anyone to talk you out of living a big life. Furthermore, people talk to you from the filters through which they see their own lives, not from the truth of how you can live your life. Note to Myself: Never ask for permission to be your authentic self.

The Lone Ride Home

Merging into traffic on interstate I-80, I smiled as the familiar breeze blew across my face. Jill Scott was blaring through the speaker, "Living my life like it's golden." Bikers often say, "Ride It like you stole it." Yes, I did, all the way back to Las Vegas. Maybe I am a bad-ass! Today I'm still riding and enjoying the breeze against my cheeks. I'm also passionate about coaching and mentoring women to "Ride it like they stole it!"

Judy-Ann Davis Young

Judy-Ann Davis Young is a native Alaskan. She spent more than 23 years working for BP Oil Company on the Trans-Alaska pipeline, where she was a poster child for women in nontraditional rolls. Young hung up her hardhat and steel-toe boots to relocate to Las Vegas, Nev., with her husband, Eddie Young. Young has a bachelor's degree in human resources and education from Alaska Pacific University and a master's degree in consciousness studies from Holmes Institute. Young is an ordained minister and serves as an outreach minister in Nevada.

Young is a Renaissance woman who has hiked through the rainforest in Ghana, West Africa; walked on the Great Wall of China; and participated in the 50th Anniversary of the Selma to Montgomery Freedom March. Young has also gazed upon the vastness of the Grand Canyon and has ridden her motorcycle across 35 states. In July 2021, Young received a proclamation

RIDE IT LIKE YOU STOLE IT!

from LaToya Cantrell, mayor of New Orleans, for organizing the Harriet Tubman to Kamala Harris Tail of the Dragon Legacy Tour. She led a group of women motorcyclists to Robbinsville, N.C., to ride the challenging "Tail of the Dragon," an 11-mile stretch of highway featuring 318 curves. Sports car drivers and motorcycle enthusiasts consider the stretch a mecca and an epic ride.

Young is deputy commander of the Buffalo Soldier Motorcycle Club Las Vegas Post, where she enjoys teaching Buffalo Soldier and Juneteenth history to the public.

Young is passionate about life coaching and being a certified grief recovery specialist. Her Motto is "I am the only one; no one came here to be me!"

You may reach JudyAnn at
Email: judyannyoung@gmail.com
IG: judyann_speaks

CHASING 100

Cash Abundance: More Than Money

By Katrina Fitten

I'll never forget the feeling of standing on the edge of giving up. The years of relentless hustle in my business and the constant battle to stay afloat all felt like too much. I had fought my way out of personal financial chaos—scraping by on payday loans, hiding from bill collectors, watching my bank account dip into the red month after month. I knew what it was like to be buried under a mountain of debt, to feel the shame of not being able to make ends meet, to cry myself to sleep wondering how I'd ever get out of the hole I was in.

But I didn't give up. I knew I needed a fresh start, a way to turn all the pain I'd been through into something meaningful, something that could change lives. That's when New Day For You Financial was born. It wasn't just a business; it was my new beginning. It was the lifeline I had been searching for—the opportunity to take everything I had learned from my struggles and use it to empower others. I was determined to make sure that no other woman would have to face the kind of financial despair I had endured. Frankly, I believed with every fiber of my being that this business was my calling.

A few years into the business, however, everything felt like it was crumbling. The growth I'd dreamed of wasn't happening. Cash flow was unpredictable; invoices took forever to get paid. I was dipping into my personal savings to pay some business expenses, and I was emotionally and mentally exhausted from trying to do it all on my own without a team.

How did it come to this? After all, I had overcome, why was my business now failing? The same strategies that saved me personally weren't working in my business. I had a degree in economics, yet I couldn't seem to figure it out. I watched others on social media making it look easy, while I was drowning in self-doubt, feeling like a fraud, yes, an imposter.

I was at the breaking point, seriously considering walking away from everything I'd built. But then something happened that changed everything.

It was an action that is so simple and yet so difficult: I finally opened up to a mentor— someone I trusted, someone who had walked the path before me. I laid it all out, the struggles, the fears, the sense of defeat that had been gnawing at me. And what was shared was truly a revelation. "You're not alone," my mentor said. "You'd be surprised how many business owners are fighting the same battle." Then, the truth bomb was dropped regarding a statistic that hit me like a ton of bricks: 82% of businesses fail because of cash- flow issues. The very struggle I was drowning in was one of the most common reasons businesses go under. It was like the elephant in the room that no one wanted to acknowledge.

But more than that, this solution hadn't even been considered: business funding. It's a strategy that 95% of female entrepreneurs overlook. I'd been so focused on doing everything the "right" way, on bootstrapping and using my own resources, that I'd never stopped to think there might be another way—a better way.

And that's when everything changed.

The first lesson I learned was about mindset. I had to completely rethink my relationship with money in my business. The strategies that had helped me claw my way out of personal debt had also planted seeds of limiting beliefs. I'd been taught to fear debt, to see borrowing as something negative, something to avoid at all costs. And that mindset was strangling my busi-

CASH ABUNDANCE: MORE THAN MONEY

ness. I'd been treating business like it was my personal finances, when in reality, they are two entirely different animals. In business, borrowed money isn't just debt—it's an asset. It's a powerful tool to be leveraged to generate returns far beyond what you could achieve on your own. It's the catalyst that allows you to do more, to do it better, and to do it faster.

I had to shift my thinking from "debt is bad" to "debt is a tool" that can be used in business. This shift didn't just change how I viewed borrowing; it changed everything. Suddenly, I could see opportunities where before I had seen only obstacles. Business funding wasn't just a lifeline—it was a launchpad.

The second lesson was about the power of expertise. I was exhausted from trying to be everything in my business—CEO, marketer, sales manager, accountant, customer service rep, all rolled into one. I was burning the candle at both ends, staying up late on YouTube University watching tutorials, trying to teach myself everything I needed to know. But here's the truth: if you want to go faster, you have to hire a master. Business funding opened doors. It gave me the ability to invest in multiple opportunities, giving me access to experts who had already walked the path, who knew the pitfalls, who had already scraped their knees and had the scars to prove it. They helped me avoid mistakes that could have cost me everything.

The third lesson was about strategic relationships and partnerships. For so long, I had prided myself on being a self-made woman. I had pulled myself up by my bootstraps, and I thought that meant I had to do everything on my own. But I was wrong. Business is about relationships—real, genuine connections with others who are on the same journey. When I started opening up, when I began investing in mentorships and joining communities of like-minded entrepreneurs, everything started to shift. I found people who understood the struggles, who had been where I was, and who could offer not just advice, but support.

Without these relationships, I would still be stuck. These strategic relationships and partnerships are the backbone of my business, the foundation that keeps me strong even when things get tough.

These lessons have fundamentally shaped my business. They've empowered me to create a community of women entrepreneurs and strategic business partners who are on the path to becoming first-generation millionaires through their businesses. We leverage funding to open doors that might otherwise remain closed, and we've built a network of experts who share their wisdom and expertise. No one in our community is ever alone, and we're taking money off the table as a reason why they can't succeed. Over the past year, we've provided over $1 million in business funding, helping entrepreneurs fund their clients' high- ticket programs and supporting more and more women on their entrepreneurial journeys every day.

Here is what I want you to take away from this: You don't have to struggle in silence. You don't have to be on an island by yourself. There are tools and resources out there—like business funding—that can help you break through the barriers that are holding you back. Don't let cash-flow issues stop you from reaching your full potential. Don't let limiting beliefs keep you from taking your business to the next level. Leverage Other People's Money, O.P.M.). Use these lessons to fuel your growth, to build the thriving business you've always dreamed of.

It's time to stop just surviving.
It's time to start thriving.

CASH ABUNDANCE: MORE THAN MONEY

Katrina Fitten

Katrina Fitten is a certified master financial coach, business strategist and accomplished author, using her decade of experience in entrepreneurship to help women entrepreneurs achieve financial independence and success through their businesses. As the visionary CEO of New Day For You Financial, she leads a dedicated team that provides strategic business funding solutions and financial education, helping clients break free from financial constraints and build the dream business that will launch their financial empires.

Under her leadership, New Day For You Financial has become a trusted partner for coaches, consultants and small business owners, offering tailored financial services and expert guidance on leveraging Other People's Money (O.P.M.) to fuel business growth. In the last year alone, Katrina and her team have successfully funded over $1 million, supporting a growing *community of women entrepreneurs on their path to becoming first-generation millionaires.*

Katrina's clients rave about her deep knowledge, personalized approach and unwavering commitment to their success. They describe her as a catalyst for change, a mentor who empowers them to dream bigger and achieve more. With a focus on delivering tangible results and fostering long-term growth, Katrina and her team are dedicated to creating a legacy of abundance for generations to come.

You may contact Katrina at
contact@newdayforyoufinancial.com (email);
@moneycoachkatrinafitten (Instagram);
newdayforyoufinancial.com (website);
or by calling 888.633.7460.

Drowning In Debt — Discovering the Dream of Determination

By Dr. Lorie A. L. Nicholas

Have you ever had your biggest dream, the one you have chased for so long, spiral into a nightmare—and there's no one to help you?

Imagine the place you call home—a sanctuary where you've built your life, invested your dreams and created countless memories. Now imagine that sanctuary slipping away, bit by bit, with every passing day.

In 2005, when I took the plunge into home ownership, I couldn't have been happier. I'd carefully weighed my options and had taken into consideration a mixed bag of advice from family and friends — some said that buying a home was a great investment, and others believed that buying a home was a waste of money. I decided to take the leap. I bought a one-bedroom condo and was pursuing the American Dream. But what lay just ahead would turn my dream into a nightmare.

In 2008, just three years after I'd made my home purchase, the subprime mortgage crisis hit. Interest rate hikes increased monthly payments on subprime loans, which are given to borrowers with below-average credit scores. The increase in payments made them unaffordable for many homeowners. The sudden increase in mortgage rates, combined with job losses and a slowing real estate market, led to a growing number of defaults starting in 2007 and peaking in 2010. By August 2008, over 9% of all U.S. mortgages were either delinquent or in foreclosure.

I was caught in the middle of this crisis. Though I'd spent years attending workshops to learn about home ownership, I was not immune to this disaster. My mortgage payment nearly doubled. I had no idea how I'd come up with the money to make the increased payments.

The subprime mortgage crisis affected me and millions of others, upending their lives. The crisis swept through the economy like a wildfire, leaving devastation in its wake—banks folded or were swallowed by larger institutions; businesses went bankrupt, and millions lost their jobs and homes. Mortgages, once easily handed out to people like me, were now time bombs waiting to explode. And explode they did.

My life, which I had always believed was secure, began to unravel before my eyes. I had never imagined that my world could be turned so completely upside down. I had been living paycheck to paycheck, blissfully unaware that I was walking a financial tightrope with no safety net. As long as the bills were paid, I assumed I was doing fine. But I was about to learn a harsh truth—one that would shake me to my core. As I grappled with my own nightmare, I began to hear about the horrors others were facing — neighbors losing their homes, families walking away from everything they'd worked for because their mortgage payments had skyrocketed beyond what they could afford. The news was filled with heartbreaking images of families being evicted, their belongings tossed onto the street like discarded trash. I wondered, terrified if I would be next.

I fought back the only way I knew how—by trying to refinance, trying to hold onto some semblance of control. My phone calls to the banks ended with words that had become all too familiar: "I'm sorry, Ms. Nicholas, but we are unable to help you. Your credit scores are too low, and your debt-to-income ratio is too high. Since you do not have any money, you do not qualify for our loan modification program."

I lost count of how many times I heard that response, each rejection another blow to my self-esteem. Desperation had driven me to contact every bank and mortgage company I could find, pleading for help. One bank representative displayed some empathy, advising me to apply for food stamps and pointing me to some local soup kitchens. It was as if the world had turned its back on me, leaving me to face an uncertain future alone. I couldn't escape. I was lost, drowning in a sea of debt and despair, with no lifeline in sight.

In a desperate bid to keep a roof over my head, I maxed out my credit cards, using the last of my funds to pay the mortgage. The bills piled up into a mountain of debt, while the threat of eviction, foreclosure or bankruptcy loomed closer each day. The delayed payment on my credit cards was like the first domino falling, setting off a chain reaction that would wreak havoc on my financial life. Under the new credit card guidelines, missing a payment on any account gave the credit company the authority to skyrocket my interest rates. For me, this meant that my rate of 9% shot up to a crippling 39.99%. No matter how many times I called the credit card companies for help, I was met with cold indifference. My long history as a loyal, paying customer meant nothing.

I was drowning in debt, but the financial burden was only part of the weight crushing me. The hopelessness, the shame—it was suffocating. I had always thought of myself as strong, and resilient, but this… this was different. It was like being trapped in a nightmare, where every turn led to another dead end, and the walls were closing in faster than I could find a way out. I was losing everything—my home, my dignity, my sense of self. The American Dream, once a bright sign of success, had turned into a cruel, unrelenting nightmare. I was slipping into a deep depression, and I was alone, too ashamed to let others know my painful secret.

Finally, after I made countless attempts to ask creditors for help, one creditor agreed to close my account, stop the interest from accumulating, and let me focus on paying off my balance. It was a small victory in a battle that seemed otherwise hopeless. I began to understand the true cost of financial strain. Debt was not just a number on a statement—it was a burden that people carried with them every single day, leading to anxiety, depression, and in some tragic cases, even suicide. For me, the constant stress and worry of being in debt affected every aspect of my life. I felt ashamed and embarrassed. I was a professional woman who was supposed to have it all together, yet I was unraveling.

But then, after yet another rejection from a bank, something shifted. I found myself deep in thought. I realized that I could either let this debt destroy me, or I could rise above it. I chose the latter. My faith became my anchor, giving me the strength to fight back. This time, my prayers felt different—stronger, more purposeful. As someone who had counseled thousands of clients, I asked myself how I would help a client in a similar situation, and that simple question sparked something within me. I felt a renewed strength in my faith and a determination that I would not let debt defeat me. I was going to beat it.

My heart ached for those who had lost their homes and had their lives ripped apart. I understood their pain. I could relate all too well because I was teetering on the same ledge, performing a delicate balancing act to avoid falling into eviction, foreclosure or bankruptcy. Their struggles were my struggles, and I realized that we were all in this together, all victims of a financial crisis that had left us hanging by a thread. But instead of succumbing to despair, I began to focus on recovery. What I discovered was that the path to financial recovery was grounded in the basic principles of money management. The steps I took to overcome my crisis were simple yet powerful. And as I began to climb out of the financial hole I was in, I realized that it was possible to turn my situation around. If you're in debt and feeling overwhelmed, I want you to know that you are not alone. It is possible to get out of debt and transform your financial situation.

Today, I stand on the other side of that dark chapter in my life. I emerged, getting my credit card interest rate down from 39.99% to 5%, and saving my home. I have a newfound resilience and a deeper understanding of what it means to overcome adversity. The most important lesson I learned was this: never give up on yourself or your dreams. No matter how dark things seem, no matter how many obstacles stand in your way, you have the power to change your circumstances. Stay committed; stay determined and believe that things will get better. Because they can, and they will.

One thing I would like you to remember is to stay resilient in the face of adversity. No matter how overwhelming your financial situation seems, resilience is your most powerful tool. The journey out of debt is challenging, but by staying committed and determined, you can overcome even the toughest obstacles. The foundational principles of money management—budgeting, saving and responsible spending—are essential for financial recovery. Through discovering your dream of determination, you can turn your challenges into a story of success.

I challenge you to dream big and start today chasing your 100.

Dr. Lorie A. L. Nicholas

Dr. Lorie A. L. Nicholas, CFEI, AFC, was featured in "Forbes" as one of America's Premier Experts. She is a distinguished professional with a robust background in counselling, teaching and research. Dr. Nicholas has been engaged in the field of mental health for over 30 years. With a doctorate in clinical psychology, she has presented at numerous conferences and led a variety of workshops and trainings on topics that have included mental health, stress management, race-related concerns, the criminal justice system, substance abuse, violence, incarcerated mothers and their children, and financial stress/financial literacy. Dr. Nicholas serves as an adjunct professor within the City University of New York, where she teaches a multitude of courses. Dr. Nicholas is also a certified financial education instructor and an accredited financial counselor, blending her expertise in *psychology and money to empower individuals with knowledge and skills for better mental and financial well-being. Her diverse experiences and qualifications make her a valuable resource in both academic and community settings.*

When not engaging in academic or professional pursuits, Dr. Nicholas can be found baking and decorating sweet treats or volunteering, building homes with Habitat for Humanity; helping animals get adopted with the ASPCA; and engaging in activities with The Food Networks-No Kid Hungry and GOD's Love We Deliver.

"The struggles along the way are only meant to shape you for your purpose." - Chadwick Boseman

CHASING 100

HEED THE CALL OR PLAY IT SAFE?

By Marie Yolaine Toms

Unqualified. An imposter. Too many liabilities. These thoughts stole my joy, my sense of purpose, my dreams and my voice. The worst part? I believed them.

But I didn't start out as an imposter—I was taught to be one. The word "imposter" was never used. Instead, I was taught to "play it safe." I came to America as a happy, funny, extroverted kid with my overprotective but well-meaning Haitian parents. My aunt likes to say they always had to keep an eye on me because I'd walk up to anyone, say hi and make friends. On the playground, I was usually the kickball captain. I was a confident, natural-born leader.

In the fourth grade, I played the role of Gretel in our school's production of "Hansel and Gretel." Standing on stage, I felt a rush of excitement and knew that acting was my calling. I ran home after school, brimming with enthusiasm, and told my mom, "Mom! I'm going to be an actor!"

She looked at me and said, "Ki Sa? Actress? Sa sa ye? (What is that?). No." And like the general of the Caribbean mother's army, she laid out my "play it safe" options: doctor, lawyer, engineer, nurse, or nun! I was crushed.

My dad echoed her disapproval: "You will be poor. Be safe. Don't forget; you are Haitian, you are a girl." I felt rejected and broken. My big personality shrank, and the confident leader in me was replaced by someone who would "play it safe."

My parents had their reasons. My mom often told me how hard

it was to be a woman, and my dad's stories of the racism and indignity he faced as a cab driver were crushing. They weren't bad people; they only wanted to protect me. But in trying to protect me, they unknowingly taught me to hide the real me.

After high school, I did what was expected. I went to college. I wanted to major in theater/TV arts, but I played it safe and chose communications and business management. I found a safe job behind the camera, far away from the spotlight that once called to me. I became an expert at dimming my light. I built fences to keep others out, not realizing they became the bars of my own prison.

For years, I harbored resentment toward my parents, believing they had stolen my joy and kept me from my dreams. It took time, difficult conversations and therapy to understand that they weren't withholding anything from me. Their dreams, voices and sense of purpose were stolen by playing it safe. They were suspicious of this new country, and instead of preparing me for it, they isolated me. I knew nothing about managing myself, handling my finances or being an adult. In trying to fill the void left by my suppressed dreams, I made terrible financial decisions and spiraled into debt.

They say God doesn't force your will, but he does know how to make you willing. By 2003, I was buried under thousands of dollars in student loans, credit card and medical bill debt. I had tried to get out of debt before only to fall back in twice as deep. I prayed, read books, created spreadsheets—yet something was missing.

In 2006, a friend asked me to be her accountability partner because she was overspending. I thought, "Lord, why did you put me on her heart when you know I have an 'unhealthy' relationship with a certain shoe store?"

It triggered the time I ruptured my Achilles tendon and was rushed to the ER only to be told, "You have no insurance. We can't serve you." I'd just graduated but had no job, money or savings. I couldn't even do self-pay. I was humiliated and terrified I would be crippled for the rest of my life. No one ever taught me

HEED THE CALL OR PLAY IT SAFE?

how to save, budget or pay bills. I had to teach myself.

Despite feeling unqualified, I remembered how I invested in financial literacy, faced my financial trauma and climbed out of debt. This time, I chose not to play it safe. I went home and prepared to be the best money coach and accountability partner ever. I created a full curriculum, shared it with my friend, who then shared it with her sister and others, and the Financial Freedom Workshop (FFW) was born.

Since then, many who came to the FFW burdened with debt are debt-free or are on their way. This is my passion, ministry and business. I teach what I overcame. Jeremiah 29:11 is true: "I know the plans I have for you, not to harm you but to give you hope and a future." True partnership with God is serving people.

Meanwhile, my acting dream came true when an on-air host didn't show up at my job. The director was scrambling for a replacement, looked at me and asked, "Can you fill in?"

I said, "Sure, if there's no one else," but inside, I screamed, "I'm ready for my close-up!"

I nailed it! Gretel was still alive. I started auditioning and booked a role in a stage play at the Kennedy Center. That success led me to pack my bags and move to New York to be an actor. On opening night of my first off-Broadway play, my mom and dad were in the audience. I did my thing. My mom came backstage, walked up to me and asked, "You're an actor now?"

Inside, I reverted to that defenseless kid, but outside, I was grown. I'd learned how not to play it safe. I pulled my shoulders back and, with my whole chest, said, "Yes, Mommy, I am an actor now."

She looked at me and said, "You did a good job." I almost passed out.

On January 12, 2010, an earthquake struck my homeland like a meteor. In 35 seconds, over 316,000 people, including some of my family, were dead. Watching the news, I saw an elderly woman lying on the ground, writhing in pain. The back of her body was fully exposed. I screamed at the TV, "Why doesn't someone cover her up? She's someone's wife, someone's grandmother! Doesn't anyone care about human dignity anymore? God, someone needs to go and do something!"

Suddenly, I heard a quiet voice inside me say, "You go." I argued, "Lord, I clearly said someone needs to go do something. I'm not qualified! I'm not a doctor, nurse or engineer. I don't have a nonprofit." Silence. I could have played it safe and donated. Donating might have satisfied me, but it would never have fulfilled me. I heeded the call, jumped without a net and left my safe job. I was on the next plane home, terrified and excited at the same time.

I networked, created partnerships, took leadership courses and founded my nonprofit, Community2Community (C2C). Today, C2C is a thriving service and development organization working with over 1,200 families in vulnerable communities to restore their lives. I answered the call instead of playing it safe. I am called and qualified. I am a restorer of dignity and attract people with a heart for generosity to do the same.

Had I played it safe, I would have never moved to NYC to pursue acting. I would have never left my job to start Community2Community. I would have never faced my money trauma, gotten out of thousands of dollars in debt, using my mistakes to empower others as a money mindset coach. It's not how you start that matters; it's how you finish. I started in the light and got knocked into the shadows. I fought my way back to the light. I faced my fears of rejection and the need for validation. Playing it safe might satisfy you, but it will not fulfill you. It takes more energy to be an imposter than it does to be your true self. The imposter still whispers to me to play it safe, but the less I listen, the more it fades.

I am a natural-born organizer, teacher and encourager. These are the gifts, talents and abilities God gave me to work with while I'm here. It took years to embrace each one, and now I hold them close. God created me female, Black, and Haitian. I used to think these three attributes were liabilities. Now I know they were always assets. He knew that only in this package could I fight to defeat the "play it safe" mindset to become

HEED THE CALL OR PLAY IT SAFE?

the overcomer I am today. I know I'm not the only one, so I'm shouting it from the mountaintops: Don't play it safe. No one successful ever played it safe. We are not created to play it safe; we are created to heed the call. I am built to lead and serve as an actor, CEO and coach.

Heeding the call isn't about following a passion—it's about recognizing that you were created for something greater. It's about the lives you will impact for good. If you feel the call, don't wait to be qualified. Don't play it safe. Heed the call. You were made for this moment.

MarieYolaine Toms

MarieYolaine Toms is a dynamic speaker and passionate financial empowerment coach, dedicated to helping individuals transform their relationship with money and achieve financial freedom. With a background in communications and business management, she combines practical financial education with a deep understanding of the emotional and psychological aspects of money management.

Born in Haïti and raised by immigrant parents, MarieYolaine learned early the mindset of "playing it safe." However, her journey led her to break from this mindset, embracing her true calling to serve and empower others. She is the founder of the Financial Freedom Mastermind, where she guides clients through the process of overcoming financial trauma, building financial literacy and achieving debt-free living.

HEED THE CALL OR PLAY IT SAFE?

MarieYolaine is also the CEO+FireStarter of Community-2Community (C2C), a thriving service and development nonprofit working with vulnerable communities in Haïti to restore their lives. C2C's vision is Development With Dignity. Their work is impacting over 1,200 families.

In addition to her coaching and nonprofit work, MarieYolaine is a passionate advocate for the importance of health and wellness, incorporating principles from her Pilates practice into her teachings. She is known for her ability to connect with clients on a deep level, offering support, encouragement and the tools they need to succeed.

When she's not coaching or leading her nonprofit, MarieYolaine enjoys acting, having performed at the Kennedy Center and in national commercials. Her life's mission is to help others heed their call, embrace their unique gifts and live a life of significance. She credits her achievements to Luke 1:37.

You may reach MarieYolaine at www.FocusedFire.Life.

CHASING 100

Every Setback is a Setup for a Comeback

By Michelle Richburg

The day I was fired was one of the most devastating moments of my life. I had dedicated myself to my career, pouring every ounce of energy into my work. My career wasn't just what I did; it was who I was.

Losing that job wasn't just a professional setback; it felt like a personal failure. The feeling of betrayal was immediate and overwhelming. I remember sitting in the HR office, trying to process the words being spoken to me, but everything felt like a blur. How could this be happening to me? I had given so much, sacrificed so much, and in return, I was left with nothing.

That night, I cried myself to sleep, overwhelmed by the fear of what was to come. How was I going to support my son? How would I keep our home? The anxiety was crippling, and the future felt bleak. I even started planning to sell my house because I couldn't see a way out. The thought of losing the place where I had raised my son, where we had built so many memories, was heartbreaking. My sense of identity was shattered, and with it, my confidence. I had always been the strong one, the one who had everything together, but now, I felt completely lost.

As if losing my job wasn't enough, I was dealt another crushing blow just a few months later. I was in a serious relationship, engaged, and planning a future with someone I thought I could trust. But without warning, he disappeared—literally vanished from my life. He stopped answering calls, stopped showing up;

it was as if he had been erased from existence. The heartbreak was immense. I had been blindsided, and the emotional toll was enormous. I was left to grapple with the emotional wreckage, feeling abandoned and alone.

During those months, my mental state was fragile. Every day was a struggle just to get out of bed. I was overwhelmed by a sense of failure and loss, questioning everything about myself—my worth, my future and my ability to ever find happiness again. It felt like the world was closing in on me, and I couldn't see a way out. I spent countless nights lying in bed, staring at the ceiling, wondering how everything had gone so wrong. My mind was a constant whirlwind of "what ifs" and "if onlys."

My son, Adrian, was in high school in Connecticut, and every morning, I would drive him there and back, all the while feeling like I was going through the motions of a life that no longer made sense. The drives were long, and it was during these quiet moments that the reality of my situation would hit me the hardest. I wasn't going to work—I didn't have a job to go to. I was a 48-year-old woman in sweatpants, driving back home to an uncertain future.

Despite the darkness, I wasn't completely alone. I had a strong support system that I leaned on heavily during this time. My pastor, a dear friend from Syracuse, would visit me every Wednesday without fail. He would take me out to lunch, sit with me by the water and just be there. His presence was a lifeline, a reminder that I wasn't alone in my struggles.

Those afternoons by the water became a sanctuary for me, a place where I could let down my guard and just be.

My mentor, Dorene, also played a crucial role. She would meet with me every two weeks, pushing me to list my skills, my accomplishments and my connections. She made me see that I had value, even when I couldn't see it myself. But despite their support, I still felt lost, disconnected from the person I used to be. I would often sit with Dorene, a notebook in hand, trying to write down what she asked of me, but the words felt hollow. It was as if the person she was describing wasn't me anymore.

EVERY SETBACK IS A SETUP FOR A COMEBACK

As the months dragged on, I knew I had to do something to change my situation. But fear held me back—fear of rejection, fear of failure, fear of the unknown. I was terrified to reach out to my former contacts, terrified to put myself out there again. But I also knew that I couldn't stay in the same place forever. I had to take a risk, even if it meant facing my worst fears.

One day, I finally mustered the courage to reach out to James and Kevin, two people who had been pivotal in my career. I was terrified, but I knew I had to do something to change my situation. To my surprise, they hired me as their business manager within seconds of our meeting. It was a shock—a moment of validation that I desperately needed. But even then, the fear didn't fully dissipate. I still struggled with self-doubt, still questioned whether I was truly capable of succeeding on my own.

Those first few weeks working with James and Kevin were nerve-wracking. Every task felt like a test, and I was constantly worried that I would let them down. But as I threw myself into the work, something incredible happened: I started to remember why I loved what I did. The challenges that once seemed insurmountable became opportunities for growth, and with each small success, my confidence began to rebuild.

But the biggest revelation came later, when I was watching Oprah talk about living your best life. It was like a light switch went on in my mind. I understood, deep in my soul, that I was not defined by my past, by my failures or by the people who had let me down. I was defined by my resilience, by my ability to rise above the challenges that life had thrown at me.

I began to see that every setback was an opportunity for growth. Every failure was a chance to learn, to reevaluate and to come back stronger. I realized that I had a unique gift to offer the world—a gift that wasn't tied to a job or a title, but to who I was as a person.

I am the gift. This experience showed me that my value is not tied to anyone or anything outside of myself. My value comes from who I am—the woman God created me to be—and the purpose he has set out for me. This realization has given me the confidence to move forward, to embrace new challenges and to continue growing into the person I was meant to be.

I remember sitting down with my vision board, something I had started years ago but had neglected during the dark times. I began to fill it with new dreams, new goals and a new vision for my future. I realized that I wasn't just surviving — I was thriving. And I was determined to keep pushing forward, to keep chasing my 100.

Today, I look with pride at the life I've built. I've gone from a place of uncertainty and fear to a place of confidence and success. I've built a business that I'm proud of, one that allows me to work with incredible clients and make a real impact. I've also built a life that I love, one that includes travel, new experiences and the joy of knowing that I'm living out my purpose.

But I didn't get here by taking shortcuts. I got here by doing the work, by being relentless in my pursuit of excellence and by refusing to settle for anything less than what I knew I was capable of. That's what "Chasing 100" is all about striving to be the best version of yourself, no matter what obstacles come your way.

Throughout this journey, my faith has been a constant anchor. There were times when I didn't know how I was going to make it, but I always knew that God had a plan for me. One of my favorite Bible verses is Jeremiah 29:11, which says, "For I know the plans I have for you," declares the Lord, "plans to prosper you and not to harm you, plans to give you hope and a future." This verse has been a source of comfort and strength for me, reminding me that even in the darkest times, there is a purpose to my pain.

As I continue to chase my 100, I know that there will be more challenges ahead. But I also know that I'm equipped to handle them. I've been through the fire, and I've come out stronger on the other side. I'm not the same person I was 13 years ago—I'm better. And I'm ready to keep pushing, keep growing and keep chasing that next level of excellence.

If there's one thing I want you to take away from this chapter, it's this: You have the power to overcome any obstacle. You have

EVERY SETBACK IS A SETUP FOR A COMEBACK

the strength to rise above your circumstances and create the life you want. But it's not going to be easy. It's going to require hard work, resilience and a willingness to push past your comfort zone. But if you're willing to do that, the rewards are limitless.

Michelle Richburg

    Michelle Richburg is widely recognized as the "Money Mastermind Behind Biggest Names in Music" from her 30-year career in financial services.

    As CEO of Richburg Enterprises, Michelle is dedicated to providing a comprehensive range of services and revenue-generating opportunities that positively impact the lives and legacies of her clients.

    Her outstanding business and philanthropic contributions have earned her the following recognition:

- The Buddy White Project Community Service Award: 2024
- Billboard Top Business Manager four consecutive years in a row: 2020, 2021, 2022, and 2023
- Billboard "Women in Music" award: 2023
- Billboard Hip Hop and R&B Power Player List: 2021, 2022

EVERY SETBACK IS A SETUP FOR A COMEBACK

- *Faculty member for Warner Music Group's first Global DEI Institute*
- *Recording Academy, Professional Member: 2021*
- *New York State, Congressional Proclamation, Jamaal Bowman*
- *New York State Senate 36th District Proclamation*
- *Westchester County Board of Legislators Proclamation*
- *Office of the Mayor, City of Mount Vernon, Proclamation*
- *New York State Assembly Citation*

You may reach Michelle at www.richburgenterprisesllc.com.

CHASING 100

A Journey Back to Myself

By Star Bobatoon, Esq.

It was late on a Tuesday night when the phone rang, and a family friend asked my mother, "Can you get Star out to California by Friday for an audition?" By the next night, I was on a plane soaring toward what felt like destiny.

I was 16 years old, and I had been acting as long as I could remember. Acting was in my blood, part of my very being. Stage plays, movies, TV — I had done it all. But this was different. This was the break I had been waiting for—a lead role in a prime-time television show. It was the culmination of years of dreaming and thousands of hours training and preparing. I had been paying my dues, and this was my moment. I was too excited.

What I didn't know was that the role had already been promised to Janet Jackson. Contracts were ready, sitting on her agent's desk. All she had to do was sign them. But after I auditioned, they gave the part to me.

I had just won the lead role over Janet Jackson! Getting that role was an amazing opportunity, and it should have been the start of something extraordinary. But instead, it marked the beginning of a detour — a detour from my potential, away from my destiny. After I landed that role, a lot of tension and stress starting building in my family. I assumed the stress was because of my being in the spotlight. By the end of the second year of the show, I was sad, lonely and miserable. What should have been a dream come true turned into a nightmare.

I decided that it just wasn't worth it. So, I walked away from the stage, from acting and from the dream that had driven me for so long. I muted my voice. I dimmed my light and turned my back on my destiny, on who I was and the person I could become.

Years passed, and life was good—at least on the surface. I got married, had children and became an attorney. I was living what many would consider a successful life. But deep down, I knew if living my full potential was 100, I was barely getting by at 75.

I knew something wasn't right, but I wasn't willing to do anything about it. I had a good life: I was working in a high-profile law firm; my husband and I had double-six-figure incomes; we had the nice house, fancy cars, vacations, kids in private school. Life was good. I had every reason to be happy, every reason to be grateful for what I had. Nothing was wrong, but something wasn't right.

One of my mentors said that when you are too afraid to make a move in your life, life will move on you. And that's exactly what happened to me.

In the span of a year, everything in my life turned upside down. My father died; my job went away, and my marriage fell apart. All the anchors that had been keeping me grounded were gone, and I spiraled into a deep depression.

When a good friend invited me to attend a seminar, I went. I had nothing to lose. I found myself sitting in the audience, watching amazing speakers command the stage. As they spoke, I saw their passion, their conviction for what they were doing, and I saw the positive impact on the audience. And suddenly I remembered the part of myself that had been left behind when I walked away from acting.

At that moment, I saw my 100. The speakers on that stage reminded me of the light I had dimmed, the voice I had muted. And I knew then that I had to take a risk. I had to chase my 100.

It wasn't easy. I had a family and responsibilities and had been hiding for 25 years. But I couldn't ignore the call any longer. I couldn't continue to live a life that wasn't fully mine. So, I took the leap, made the sacrifices to reclaim my voice, my

A JOURNEY BACK TO MYSELF

light, my destiny.

I ended up training and speaking internationally with motivational icon Les Brown, and I ran his speaker training program. I became the number-one trainer in a national training company. I have spent over 9,000 hours on stages here and abroad. I've had the privilege of speaking on stages with some amazing people, including former first lady Michelle Obama. I reclaimed my voice and embraced my light. I left 75 behind to forever "chase 100."

I am Star Bobatoon, and I invite you to embrace your inner light and be the star you were born to be.

Star Bobatoon, Esq.

What brings Star Bobatoon the greatest joy is the opportunity to coach and empower professionals to amplify their voices and illuminate their light so they can shine like the stars they were born to be. After 30-plus years of experience as a performer on stage and screen, as an award-winning keynote speaker and top performing trainer, she recognizes that too many have made the choice to dim their lights and mute their voices in order to navigate their lives. She views this as a tragedy, and it is the reason she is dedicated to work with individuals, teams and organizations to sharpen their communication and performance skills so they can deliver compelling messages that amplify their influence and their impact.

In order to master her communication and training skills, Star trained and shared the stage with motivational icon Les Brown and ran his speaker training program. She honed her skills as a contract trainer for a national training company, becoming the top trainer in sales and performance. Her clients include Toyota Motors, The Washington Nationals and World Wildlife Foundation. She has been honored to share the stage with Lisa Nichols, Suze Orman and former first lady, Michelle Obama. As vice president of programs with Andy Henriquez, she works with clients to elevate their lives and their businesses through the power of story.

While she is proud of the work she has done, nothing makes her prouder than watching clients embrace their inner light and become the stars they were meant to be.

You may reach Star at star@Starbobatoon.com or www.starbobatoon.com.

CHASING 100

The Unseen Path to Purpose

By Dr. Torrey Montgomery

The Unexpected Calling

Growing up, I was constantly told that I would one day be a preacher. Let me tell you, that's something that I never even considered. I figured that people said it only because my dad was a pastor. He was absolutely phenomenal, but I wanted to be a touring musician and producer. If that didn't work, my plan was to be a professional fighter. I envisioned myself becoming a UFC world champion or something along those lines. It's funny how our plans often don't align with God's plan.

The Journey Begins: A Musician's Dream

After moving to Oklahoma City, Okla., I began playing keyboard for a very progressive church and served as the assistant music and arts director. We were producing albums and even preparing for a tour. It felt like I had finally made it; my dreams were about to come true. One Sunday morning, as I was playing the keyboard before church, my pastor walked in, pointed at me, and said, "It's on you today." Confused, I ran into his office and asked, "What's on me?" He simply replied, "I think you're ready. It's time for you to bring the word—you're preaching today."

The fear that came over me was unexplainable, but I accepted the challenge. Drawing from my karate experience, where I knew how to break boards, I decided to incorporate that into my sermon. I broke boards and preached a message about the power of breakthrough.

Little did I know that day would ignite something within me that would change the course of my life.

The Defining Moment: Discovering My Calling

That unexpected moment became the catalyst for a passion I never knew existed. I became passionate about speaking and empowering people. That day marked the beginning of a journey I never saw coming. I finally found my calling.

This moment answered three of the most vital questions in life:
- Who are you?
- Why are you here?
- Where are you going?

It's often said that we all have defining moments, and these moments either define us or we define them. For me, this was a defining moment that led me to launch a 21st-century church, training leaders from all over the world to become high-capacity leaders. Ironically, I was doing the very thing I once said I would never do. It's true what they say—never say never.

The Real Challenge:
Endurance Over Enthusiasm

Through this journey, I learned that starting is always the easiest part. The real challenge lies in the endurance to keep going. As a pastor, coach and leader of leaders, I hear one word more frequently than you could imagine. This one word has stopped ministries from moving forward, caused businesses to shut down and prevented gifted people from realizing their true potential. Even high-level athletes have fallen prey to its deceptive power. This word has disappointed teams and communities, and I might even say that it has been the single-most destructive enemy to destiny.

You're probably wondering what that word is. Before I reveal it, let me ask you a few questions:
- What would it mean to you if you fulfilled your dream?
- What would change in your life if your vision came to pass?

THE UNSEEN PATH TO PURPOSE

How would your life transform if your ministry became everything you believed it could be? If your business started to thrive, and you reached your financial goals?

These are important questions. I'm sure your life would change significantly if you knew there was no possibility of failure—you would go all in with no thought of retreat. Now, what if I told you that this one word, which many of us have felt, is not real? It's imagined, and with the right strategy, it will never trouble you again.

So, what is this word? It's "burnout." Every leader at some point will say they have felt this somewhere in their journey, and unfortunately, too many have accepted it as their reality. Year after year, sometimes even month after month, someone comes into my office and says, "I think I'm going to quit." My immediate question is always, "Why do you feel you need to step down?" Almost without exception, the response is, "I'm just burnt out."

After over a decade of leading and empowering people to walk in their calling and live out their purpose, I've learned that burnout is never really burnout. Burnout is just a way of expressing an internal barrier that one has not been able to overcome. So let me say this again—burnout is not real. It's only imagined.

Overcoming Burnout: The Three R's

Burnout. It's a word that has become so common in our fast-paced world, where people seem to be chasing after something—success, recognition, fulfillment—but often find themselves feeling drained and ready to quit. I've seen it stop ministries dead in their tracks, shut down businesses and derail people from their true potential. I've even seen it take down high-level athletes, people who've pushed their bodies and minds to the limit, only to find themselves standing at the edge, wondering if it's all worth it.

But here's the thing: burnout isn't real. At least, not in the way we think it is. It's not some insurmountable wall that we slam into at full speed. No, burnout is an illusion—a way of expressing the internal barriers we haven't figured out how to overcome yet. And like any illusion, once you see it for what it is, you can begin to dismantle it. In my journey, I've learned that overcoming burnout comes down to three critical steps: Realign, Redefine, and Relaunch.

Realign: Adjust Your Focus

When I first stepped into that pulpit, completely unprepared and scared out of my mind, I had to realign my focus on the spot. My plans, my dreams of becoming a touring musician or a UFC champion—they didn't align with the path God had for me. It wasn't until I stepped back and took a hard look at where I was and why I was there that I realized I needed to shift my focus.

Realignment isn't just about changing directions; it's about making sure that your actions, your energy and your time are all invested in what really matters. It's about asking yourself, "Am I still in sync with my purpose?" If you're feeling burnt out, maybe it's time to check your alignment. Maybe it's time to focus on the bigger picture again and make sure that you're on the path that God has set before you.

Redefine: Reassess Your Goals

As I continued on this unexpected journey into ministry, I had to redefine what success looked like for me. My goals of producing albums and touring the world shifted into something I never imagined—launching a church, training leaders and empowering people. Burnout often comes when we're chasing goals that no longer fit who we've become.

Redefining your goals means taking stock of where you are right now and where you want to go. It's about being honest with yourself and letting go of the things that no longer serve you. Just because something was your dream yesterday doesn't mean it's your destiny today. If you're feeling burnt out, maybe it's time to redefine what success means for you and to set your sights on something that truly resonates with your current reality.

Relaunch: Start Fresh with Renewed Energy

That day when I broke boards and preached my first sermon, I didn't just step into a pulpit—I relaunched my life. What started as a terrifying moment turned into the beginning of a journey I never expected. But I didn't stop there. Over the years, I've had to keep relaunching, over and over again, as I faced new challenges and new opportunities.

Relaunching isn't about forgetting the past or pretending that burnout never happened. It's about taking everything you've learned—the struggles, the setbacks, the breakthroughs— and using it to fuel a new beginning. It's about stepping back into the ring with a fresh perspective, a clear vision and the energy to keep fighting for what matters.

The Power to Overcome

Burnout doesn't have to be the end of your story. It can be the beginning of something new, something better than you ever imagined. When you feel that exhaustion creeping in, when you start questioning whether you can keep going, remember that you have the power to realign, redefine and relaunch.

You've got the power to change your narrative, just like I did, to step back, refocus and step forward with renewed strength and purpose. This journey isn't over. In fact, the best is yet to come. Your defining moment is waiting—now it's up to you to define it.

So, the next time you feel like you're about to hit that wall, remember: it's not real. It's just an illusion, and you've got everything you need to break through it. Just like I did.

Dr. Torrey Montgomery

Dr. Torrey Montgomery's purpose in life is to help people come into "full expression" of who they are. Over the past decade Torrey has used his voice in the spaces of education, government, corporate settings and ministry. He has traveled abroad to several countries teaching the message of the Kingdom and training leaders. He has focused on the science of getting unstuck and helping people transition into new paradigms in their mindsets. He has been featured on various television and radio broadcasts. Torrey and his wife, Janelle, are lead pastors of Ignite Church Global in Oklahoma City, Okla.

Coach Torrey lives by the saying, "Your best days are not behind you. They're not in front of you. They are inside of you."

You may reach Coach Torrey at imotivatetolead@gmail.com.

Made in the USA
Middletown, DE
07 February 2025